APPROACH

APPROACH:

The Rejection-Free Way for Marketers to Reach Your Ideal Clients, Have Them Clamoring to Work with You, and Grow Your Business with Multiple Streams of Revenue.

LEE NAZAL

SOCIAVERSE PUBLISHING
www.sociaversepublishing.com

APPROACH © **2015** Lee Nazal

ISBN-13:978-0692448458 (SociaVerse Publishing)

ISBN-10:0692448454

TABLE OF CONTENTS

DEDICATION

This book is dedicated to my beautiful and supportive wife, Bernadette, who makes me a better person. Everything positive in my life, I owe to you. You opened my horizons, showed me the world, and keep my soul alive. I love you more than you'll ever know.

To Nico, my supremely talented and intelligent son. Always chase your dreams and never let anything get in the way. You remind me so much of myself in my youth. Don't be like me. You're too good to take the paths I chose for myself. Blaze your own trail. I'm proud of you, no matter what.

To Julianna, my first daughter. You are so loving, so sweet, and so bright. Your positivity and goodness make wherever you stand a beacon of light. Never change, never compromise, and be you. Your future is limitless, and so is my love for you.

To Samantha, my baby. There's a reason why everyone wants to be your friend. Your quiet demeanor belies your charisma and brilliance. You are destined for greatness no matter what you want to pursue. No matter how low I feel, you always make me happy.

PREFACE: ONE EMAIL CAN CHANGE THE WORLD

When I was in college, I wanted nothing but to be rich, so that's how I got started in my own business brokering promissory notes and receivables in the secondary market in 1996. I used the internet to market the business. I had a $10,000 investment from my father, which should have been plenty to make serious bank. Unfortunately, I blew it all, mainly because I didn't know what I was doing. It was a massive failure. As I left college and got a real job in the real world, I still wanted to be rich but the business took a back seat to my career, although any spare time I had was spent learning about marketing.

When my son was born, I quit my job in the mortgage business. We didn't have any money, so we moved into my mom's basement. This was truly rock bottom. To start making a little bit of cash, I delivered newspapers, hence my moniker of 'Paperboy'. I had to get up at 3 AM every day, including weekends and holidays, in all types of weather. It was a source of income, but I had to get another job, and I was not about to return to the mortgage industry.

My real expertise was in computers, so I was able to land a job in the IT industry. The pay was decent, but it wasn't enough to get us out of my mother's basement, so I kept the newspaper job and worked two jobs for about 2 years to save some money to buy a house.

All the while, I was learning marketing to try to make more money than I was making with the newspaper so I could quit that job. It wasn't about getting rich anymore; I just wanted a normal life. One morning, while delivering papers, I was carjacked. That's right, I was forced out of my car and my car was stolen. In the end, everything was fine, but it was a real turning point in my life. I was desperate, and something had to change.

Within a year or so of the carjacking, we had enough money to buy a house. We left the Washington, DC area, which was too expensive to live in, and moved to Atlanta, where the cost of living is lower and the weather is better. I still wanted to achieve financial independence, so I continued my marketing education. I dabbled in HTML, SEO, blogs, and even black hat.

What happened next changed my life forever.

I was once a fan of the TV show 'The Apprentice', especially when it first started. In the show's second season, the winner was a former Army Ranger, Kelly Perdew. One day in 2005, I was browsing one of my favorite sites, washingtonpost.com. Back then, the

Post had a feature where they would host interactive online chats daily with experts, dignitaries, celebrities, and other notable individuals. One such chat was with Kelly Perdew.

During that chat, I asked him what was going to happen after his year with Trump was over, and whether he would stay with Trump or move on. He answered that when his year was close to finished, they would evaluate his performance over the past year and see if it made sense to continue. Nothing really Earth-shattering. But the aura of Trump and success was very magnetic, and I felt incredibly motivated to find my own success.

Around that same time period, I was also into fitness and nutrition. I stumbled upon a Post chat with a fitness expert and Olympic champion. I followed his chat for weeks, loving every tidbit of information that he'd give. One day, it came out that he was leaving the chat scene, and the outpouring of disappointment from the readers was palpable. Someone then asked him if he had a website so that the readers would be able to continue to follow him. He responded that he didn't have one and would maybe look for help.

Still drunk with motivation from the Kelley Perdew and Apprentice vibe, I sensed this to be an incredible opportunity to land my first client. I had none at the time, and was looking for a way to break into the consulting world. That said, I was terrified. After all, he was a beloved guru, and he'd never heard of me. I had zero credibility, no real experience worth talking about, had no product, and no marketing material. The most money I had made online was through selling old guitar equipment on eBay. All of my other ventures were abject failures.

I had his email address, but I didn't know what to say, and, worse, I didn't know how he'd respond. What if he told me to go jump off a bridge? What if he told me that someone else already reached out to him? What if he didn't respond at all?

Screw it, I decided. I mustered every ounce of willpower at my disposal to paste his email address into the To: field of my Gmail account (back when you could only get one from an invite). Yes, it was from a personal Gmail account, not some self-aggrandizing corporate domain. What do I say? I thought of all kinds of slick, John Carlton-esque, renegade type of messages to send. Then I figured, You know what? I'll just be honest and speak from the heart.

Crafting the email, I said that I was a big fan of his chats, and got a lot of value from his advice; I said I'd noticed in his most recent session that he mentioned needing a website, and was wondering if we could talk about it. With my hands trembling, I clicked the Send button. That same day, he replied with his phone number, and, with that, I had my first client.

Since then, I've grown to have many clients in my stable. I earned enough additional income to allow me to travel the world. On one particular trip, we went to Fiji. It was our second trip to Fiji, the first being your typical relaxing escape to a tropical island. For this second trip, we decided to do more enriching activities rather than just lounge on the beach.

One of these activities was to visit an orphanage. Before the visit, we took a Fijian cooking class. Fijian cuisine is a fusion of Indian cooking with local ingredients like fish and tropical fruits and vegetables. It was absolutely delicious, if I do say so myself :-) We decided that, instead of devouring our new creations, we would wrap them up and take them to the orphanage. We also purchased some groceries and brought some clothes to donate.

We spent a couple of hours at the orphanage, getting to know the kids and volunteers. All of them were such beautiful people, especially the kids, who were full of life and joy, in spite of the situation they were in. They were incredibly grateful for the food. They were even more grateful that we came all the way from America and took the time to visit them. At the end of our visit, my son, who brought a soccer ball with him, gave the ball to a kid named Isaac. The look on Isaac's face was worth every penny we spent on that trip.

It is my fantasy that our visit changed the world for these children in some small but positive way. Maybe it changed Isaac's world, if only by improving his footballing skills a little. I bring you this course with the hope that it helps you reach your financial and lifestyle goals. When you reach your goals, it is my hope that you, too, will find your Isaac and change his world.

And it all starts with one email.

INTRODUCTION

What's the number one problem facing offline or local marketers today? Getting enough clients to not only sustain your business, but to thrive. In the quest to enroll new clients, however, two enormous obstacles loom large.

First, the marketplace is crowded and noisy. You are undoubtedly a quality purveyor of marketing services to your clients. However, you are in the minority. The proliferation of spammy "SEO providers" that invade our inboxes also invade those of our potential clients'. You are guilty by association, meaning your job to enroll businesses becomes quite the challenge.

Second, you are commoditized. Because of the endless buffet of options available to businesses, you are forced to compete on factors that have little to do with the results you can achieve. Whether fairly or unfairly, you will be compared to other agencies on the basis of price, location, or your hair color.

What can you do to overcome these obstacles?

The first thing you need to do is to APPROACH your ideal clients in a way that allows you to stand out against the noise. That doesn't mean you need to be louder than everyone else. It means you need to be savvier than everyone else. The effect is that you will be welcomed by your prospect to give you the opportunity to state your case as to why you deserve their dollars.

Once you accomplish attracting the attention of your prospect, you need to demonstrate a credibility and expertise that will make the decision to select you a foregone conclusion. By doing so, you render your competition irrelevant, allowing you to command premium fees and making the sales process an absolute breeze.

In this book, we cover exactly how to execute both to perfection.

Before any business decides to take you on, you'll need to make them aware of your presence. The best way I've found to do that is by cold emailing. Not exactly the sexiest of topics. Most marketers don't even give it a second thought. They buy an infoproduct that includes an email template, and they just take that template, largely unedited, blast it to the masses, and wait for the money to roll in.

But it never exactly works out that way, does it? It's tedious, it doesn't work, and it gets you flagged as spam. Then you give up on it and move on to the next shiny object.

Here's the thing... Cold emailing actually DOES work, and works very well. The problem is no one knows how to do it correctly, and it's not your fault. The gurus give you templates to send without any explanation as to how to use them, customize them, craft them, or even send them properly. Worse, many never even actually tested their own templates! They just threw something together, figured it sounded good, and pawned it off to you to test for them.

I'm telling you that cold emailing works like GANGBUSTERS, but it has to be done right. It's more effective than most other prospecting methods out there, including cold calling and direct mail, especially for online marketers looking to fill their funnels with interested local business owners.

It's not just 'traffic' being sent to a funnel, either. We tend to think of traffic as this faceless blob of an entity that's processed until money comes out. With emailing, it's actual, real human beings with whom you are engaged, and you are guiding them down the path you set for them to lead them to a sale.

I will explain, in meticulous detail, the ins and outs of cold emailing—how to do it right, what to avoid, and how to automate it so that it gets leads for you practically on autopilot. You can prospect and sell without EVER having to talk to the lead by sending them to a video or webinar. You can make it even

MORE effective by speaking ONLY with the interested prospects, instead of dealing with the 99% of people who aren't interested and would only end up hanging up on you.

After you've announced yourself to your ideal clients, you need to give them a reason why you are the superior choice. In my experience, there is one strategy that rises above all. I'm going to go over the exact steps that I've used to build a Digital Marketing Agency (DMA) that helps local and national business clients with online marketing services using the power of the printed book.

You don't have to start a DMA for this program to work for you. This is really all about getting super-hot prospects that are very interested in what you have to offer in order to make an easier sale. You can turn them into high-paying clients, flip them for affiliate profits, or any number of other ways to make money. But unlike everything else you've seen, my approach is vastly different.

I've flipped the prospecting process completely on its head. People will be begging to work with you, instead of the other way around. People will respond to your emails, instead of deleting them or marking them as spam. People will see the value and expertise you bring to them, which will make the closing process much, much easier. If this interests you, you're in the right place. Here's the best part:

The entire system is almost entirely a fill-in-the-blank, copy and paste process!

When you implement the plan, you'll build a real business that is sustainable long-term and can allow you the freedom to work and play anywhere anytime.

CHAPTER 1: THE PROBLEM WITH PROSPECTING

What's the problem with most prospecting methods?

Prospecting is the most difficult part of running a business, yet it is the most important. Prospecting is what fills up your pipeline with potential clients who want to do business with you and pay you handsomely for your services. The problem is it's not easy to find businesses that are eager to work with you.

As online marketers, most of us are loathe to prospect, mainly because:

We're afraid of rejection. Let's face it. There is a stigma attached to salespeople, whether fairly or unfairly. Make no mistake—although you are an online marketer, you are also a salesperson, and your prospects will view you as such. Once they sniff you out, they will run as far and as fast away from you as possible, and they do so by rejecting you. We don't want to hear it. At some level, we feel as if the rejection will do some damage to our being, and no matter how much we rationalize that nothing bad will happen, the fear is too debilitating to overcome inaction.

It's time consuming. Finding the right prospects is like fishing. You go to where the fish are, bait your hook, and wait until they bite. And we all know that it takes a long time before that bite comes, if it comes at all. We are used to getting things immediately, and it feels like waiting costs us money and sales.

We have Shiny Object Syndrome. When I go on vacation, I can go for weeks without checking email. When I finally do get around to checking it, I find there are literally thousands of offers in my inbox promoting the latest software, method, technique, hack, ninja, crusher, nuker, annihilator, sniper, and mastermind that's supposed to be the ultimate answer to my client-getting problems. I'll bet you experience the same. And what's worse, many of you will dump what you're trying to do with the last thing you bought to see if the shiny new thing will work even better. Meanwhile, there's no prospecting getting done, and your pipeline is dry.

We focus on the wrong things. Sometimes we feel like we need to do everything ourselves, and we try to make everything perfect before we launch anything. We spend weeks trying to find the perfect WordPress theme, playing with the latest magic plugin, researching the perfect domain and wondering whether EMDs are better, or if hyphens kill SEO. We agonize over which is better, aWeber or GetResponse or MailChimp. Or, if we have clients already, we're so caught up with fulfillment and service that we have no time for prospecting. The problem is none of these activities are revenue-generating activities. To make more money, you need to be focused on tasks that directly generate revenue, and they include prospecting.

If you fall into any or all of these traps, there is good news for you. Cold emailing is the perfect prospecting strategy. Why?

There's no rejection. When you send an email, no one can hang up on you or slam the door in your face. You might get a bounce-back, but that doesn't even register on our radar. You might get a reply back telling you to F-off. But, honestly, that doesn't really happen much, if at all, and it certainly happens much less than a rejection over the phone.

Your message gets through. If you do it right, when you send a cold email, it will make your prospect's inbox. Your message is sitting there, waiting to be read at the prospect's convenience. Contrast that with cold calling, when you can only get your message across at the moment they pick up, and, most of the time, you don't even get the chance to get your message across because they hang up too quickly. Sure, you could leave a voicemail, but voicemail is clunkier to navigate than an inbox, and, frankly, people don't even listen to them at all these days. For the same reasons, emailing is also less intrusive than calling, so you're not starting the relationship from a position of the prospect wondering why he's being interrupted.

Sending emails can be time-consuming, but there are ways to automate it (and I'm not talking about spam blasts). Voice calling can also be automated to some extent, but you are still dealing with the interruption and inconvenience factor, plus it can get expensive.

It's more convenient for the prospect. Because business owners are short on time, they can decide what to do with your message when they have time. They can also respond to you within seconds. With a phone call, it's more of a demand on his time, and he may very well dread calling back because he could get sucked into a long, salesy conversation. There's no such commitment with a reply. He's finished with it the moment he hits Send.

You have time to craft a solid message, and it is delivered the same way every time.

Before you start blasting out messages, this is what it's NOT about.

It is not spam. Like any method, email can be abused to the point of spamming. However, with cold emailing, I'll teach you how not to cross that line into spam, both in the message and in the mechanics.

It is not autoresponders. As a tool, autoresponders are meant to automate sending emails AFTER you have established some kind of relationship with your target. Cold emailing is how to establish that relationship when you don't have one already.

It is not broadcasting. You are not sending a broadcast message. In other words, you're not sending one message to many people. You are sending one message to one person on a mass scale. Subtle nuance, but an absolutely critical distinction. Get this wrong, and the game is over.

It is not something you take lightly. With cold emailing, there is very little room for error. If done incorrectly, it is ineffective at best, and outright spam at worst. I'll teach you how to walk the straight and narrow.

The cold emailing method itself is nothing extraordinary: craft an email, send it, and follow up. Really, in terms of mechanics, it's no different than any other email you send to your friends. BUT that is a very key point. As marketers, when we send email messages, cold or otherwise, it's usually in marketing-speak—hypey, salesy, pushy—and many times going for the one-shot kill. The approach to cold emailing is almost like talking to, or making, a friend, but in a slightly more formal manner. We'll go over the structure in more detail, but the method isn't complicated.

The magic is in the detail and the automation.

Here is an outline of the steps needed to make a

successful and profitable cold email campaign:

- Define your target audience based on what you're offering.

- Gather a list of prospects to email.

- Craft a message that appeals to your target audience.

- Send the message to your prospects.

- Engage with those who replied or took your desired action.

- For those who did not reply or take action, send another email and follow up, multiple times.

- Scale and automate.

Need help with growing your offline marketing business?

Visit TrajectoryChange.com today!

CHAPTER 2: THE STATISTICS

97% of cold emails are ignored. (SalesFolk)

A sobering statistic considering that it's getting harder and harder these days to get your marketing message heard above all the noise. Local business owners are bombarded by spam, cold calls, and junk mail. That's on top of the constant barrage of messages they receive from Facebook newsfeeds, Twitter feeds, website pop-ups, radio ads, TV commercials, the list goes on and on.

That means cold email is dead, right?

Not a chance! Although statistically almost no cold emails are read, consider the following:

Crain's BtoB Magazine conducted a survey of business owners. The results:

"When asked to rank different marketing activities based on time and resources spent on each, respondents put email marketing at the top, with 49 percent saying they spend more time and resources on email than on other channels. Paid search was ranked second, with 36 percent, and display ads were ranked third, with 35 percent. Social media, which enjoys a high adoption rate among B2B marketers, also gets the least amount of their time and resources, with just 29 percent saying this tactic receives the largest share of their time and resources."

B2B marketers consider emailing as their top marketing activity. It's no surprise, considering that, according to Circle Research, 42% of businesses say email is one of their most effective lead generation channels. And for B2B marketers, 88% say email is the most effective lead generation tactic.

Would they spend so much of their resources if it didn't work?

According to the Direct Marketing Association, 66% of consumers have made a purchase online as a direct result of an email marketing message.

Still not convinced?

- Marketers consistently ranked email as the single-most-effective tactic for awareness, acquisition, conversion, and retention. - Gigaom Research "Workhorses and dark horses: digital tactics for customer acquisition" (2014)

- 55% of companies generate more than 10 percent of sales from email - Econsultancy "Emailmarketing census"(2014)

- Email is almost 40x better at acquiring new customers than Facebook and Twitter - McKinsey & Company (2014)

- DMA research puts the ROI of email marketing in 2014 at US$24,93, almost double that of search advertising and better than any other direct marketing channel - DMA UK "National client email survey 2014"

So, back to the original statistic: 97% of cold emails are ignored.

How could the failure rate be so high, and yet be touted as the most effective marketing tool?

It comes down to executing emails properly. Your emails have to be different than the rest. Not only that, you have to be more persistent than the norm.

- 48% of sales people never follow up with a prospect
- 25% of sales people make a second contact and stop
- 12% of sales people only make three contacts and stop
- Only 10% of sales people make more than three contacts
- 2% of sales are made on the first contact
- 3% of sales are made on the second contact
- 5% of sales are made on the third contact
- 10% of sales are made on the fourth contact
- 80% of sales are made on the fifth to twelfth contact

Clearly, the money is in the follow-up. More specifically, the money is in multiple follow-ups. In this guide, we're going to go over how to make sure your emails don't end up as part of the 97% that are ignored, and how to properly follow up to maximize your sales.

CHAPTER 3: WHAT TO ANTICIPATE

Without a doubt, email marketing is an extremely effective prospecting method. It's really a natural fit for offline marketers. Outside of meeting in person and actually shaking someone's hand, there is no better way to approach a potential client.

Here's the thing. Many who market to local businesses tend to think that they have a problem with their service offerings and fulfillment. In other words, they jump from offering SEO to mobile marketing to social media to video marketing, and everything in between. They think that once they have the perfect product or service to offer, business owners will melt their servers to sign up for it. That's why they keep buying the next big thing—doodle video makers, mobile site generators, reputation management automators, the list is endless.

The cold, hard truth is that everyone who wants to do offline marketing or become an offline consultant already has more than enough knowledge to do the job for their clients. You already have dozens of courses on your digital shelf on how to do local SEO services, PPC services, social media services, reputation management, and scores of other services that you can offer to local businesses. You already have all the gadgets and apps you need at your disposal. You've got landing page templates, eBook templates, blog posts, and outsourcers to put it all together for you.

What's missing? You need CLIENTS! Now, all of the courses you have on offline marketing probably have a section on how to get clients. Right now, either you don't have any clients, or don't have enough clients. That will continue to be the case if you execute the wrong system, or if you execute the right system incorrectly.

You now have the right system in your hands. Cold emailing is proven. It works. It's simple. You also have in your hands the right way to execute it.

Without taking action on cold emailing, you'll continue to search for that magic bullet. While you're searching, everyone else is taking action and signing up the businesses that you could have signed.

Or you might decide that you would rather give cold calling or direct mail a shot. No problem with that. But there's no reason not to add cold emailing to your array of prospecting weapons. You will learn how to automate the process so that it runs for you all day, every day. It's an advantage over your competitors that's a real no-brainer to implement, plus you get the benefit of having that extra 'salesman' working for you tirelessly.

Once you decide that cold emailing will enable you to sign up the clients you need, and it will, you will find that the approach is a little different than what you're accustomed to. You will need to learn a different way of writing copy that is not like the typical Internet Marketing sales copy. It's not difficult, and you'll see why, but it does take some adjustment.

You'll also need to do a little bit of reconnaissance on the front end. Again, it's not difficult, it will take some adjustment, but it makes all the difference in getting higher response rates and staying out of the spam box.

Emailing is simple, and it can be made easy, but don't make the mistake of thinking it can be half-assed. It can be incredibly tempting to take shortcuts, or skip entire steps in this method. For example, you might be tempted to use some templates that came with a local marketing course. Big mistake! Not to say that those templates don't work or that they're ineffective, but everyone else uses them.

Not only that, the techniques outlined here are the very same ones used by successful Silicon Valley startups, B2B SaaS providers, and consultants just like you. Without sticking to the course, you'll end up getting zero results for your efforts with ineffective emails, or worse, end up in the spam box and get your accounts banned.

I promise you, if you skip the fundamentals, you will

not get the results you're looking for. Every step is there for a reason. If it didn't need to be there, it would not have been included. Indeed, through trial and error over tens of thousands of emails, many steps didn't make the cut. What's left here are the bare essentials to making your prospecting a big success and putting cash in your pocket.

CHAPTER 4: MINDSET

The first thing you need to learn is that your mindset is crucial to success. I realize that you want to start prospecting and building your agency right away. You might even think that you can skip over the mindset part. That is a big mistake!

Why? Because the proper mindset enables you to:

- Differentiate yourself from every other marketer out there.

- Charge higher fees.

- Get the proper results for yourself and your clients.

Don't get me wrong – I'm not going to go all Tony Robbins on you. I'm just going to go over a couple of points to help you shift your thinking.

Mindset Tip 1

Outcome-based thinking. As online marketers, we are rooted in thinking about the services we're providing; namely, SEO, social media, PPC management, mobile marketing, video marketing, and so on. Because we think this way, what ends up happening is we present ourselves to prospects this way. We say things like, "I do SEO," or "I do Facebook."

These things DO NOT matter to your prospect. They don't care about what you do. They care about their problems and what can be done to solve them. Maybe some of you say "I can get you to #1 in Google," or "I can erase negative reviews." That is closer to what I'm talking about, but it's still not quite there.

Outcome-based thinking means you are focused on the outcome that you can give your client. What does that mean? It means that in all of your communication and marketing, you need to say exactly what the client gains from working with you. And it goes deeper than "I can get you to #1 in Google." So what if you can? What does that mean to the client? What outcome can your client expect if they become #1 in Google? After all, if you can rank your client #1 for the keyword "bamboozled by daffodils," chances are it won't make any difference to their bottom line.

Instead of: "I can get you to #1 in Google," think "I can help increase your booked appointments by 31% in the next 90 days."

Instead of: "I do Facebook," or "I can update your social media profile," think "I can help engage your current and potential customers so that they become loyal to your business and keep buying from you while they completely ignore your competition."

Mindset Tip 2

There is a second mindset shift you need to make in order to be successful. I cannot overemphasize the importance of getting this part absolutely right, which is why I'm spending so much time on it. If you get this wrong, you are doomed to fail.

Think about it like this. You and every other marketer out there have access to the same tools, same templates, same offers, same website builders, etc. If you and someone else do the exact same thing, what's going to ensure your success over them? Your mindset!

So, here's the second mindset shift you must make in order to succeed:

Process vs. Results. Most of us get caught up in results. For example, we might learn some new SEO strategy, give it a try, and then we worry about the result that came from that strategy. We worry about whether we made #1 or how long it keeps taking to get there, or what else we can do to speed things up. Here's the problem with this: when we focus on the result, we ignore or modify the process to get that result. When we ignore or change the process, then you end up messing with the strategy, and it becomes different than what was originally intended.

Let me give you an example to illustrate this point. Golf is a very technical sport. Everything in your technique has to be correct, and in harmony, in order to get the ball where you want it to go. So let's say you're just starting out, and when you hit the ball off the tee, it trickles a few yards in front of you. Not the result you're looking for, right? Now, if you practice the proper technique, day in and day out, eventually you'll get better. Even if the ball is not going where you want it to go, if you keep performing the correct "process," you'll eventually get the result.

However, if you're too results-focused, you hit the ball off the tee, and it trickles a few yards. You want it to go a hundred yards. So you start messing with your swing, your approach, your weight shift, your stance, your grip, and anything else to get that hundred yards. Then you get lucky, and somehow the ball goes a hundred yards. You celebrate. But now you can't do it consistently, and you can't do anything else with the ball when it's not on the tee. Yes, you got the result, but because you modified the process, it's not repeatable or consistent.

What's the point? When you're given instructions on how to accomplish something, whether it's an SEO tactic, a cold call script or anything else, do it precisely as it's prescribed to be done, no matter what the result is.

Follow the steps exactly as outlined, whatever it is. Even if you're not getting the response you were hoping for, focus on the process, not the result. Success leaves clues. Follow the clues -- the process -- that success left behind to increase your chances of getting the result.

Understand that if your mindset isn't there, it doesn't matter what tactics you pursue. You will limit your success. Which brings me to the next tip:

The Magic Bullet

I'm going to share with you the "Magic Bullet," the secret to profitability that all of the top gurus know but aren't willing to share. That's right, they've known all along what it takes to succeed, and through all the products and services they sell you, the one thing they've been keeping to themselves is the Magic Bullet. What is the Magic Bullet? There is no damn Magic Bullet! There is no eBook, software program, video course, webinar, or anything else that's going to make you a millionaire overnight.

What no one tells you is that it takes a lot of hard work, as well as smart work, to make it happen. It's not as push-button as they make it seem. That means you have to put in effort. Honest effort. Not necessarily perfect effort. In fact, we're not going for perfection. We're going for action. Imperfect action.

If you're looking for an easy way to make thousands of dollars, this isn't it. Yes, I will share with you the steps I have taken and the lessons I have learned in order to build a six-figure consulting business for myself. But without the proper mindset (!) and the effort to put the plan into place, you're not going anywhere.

If you're not willing to do what it takes, the rest of this book, no matter what I teach you, won't matter. It doesn't matter that I share with you the actual steps I took that built a successful business. It doesn't matter that I share with you the mistakes to avoid that will help cut your learning curve to save you a ton of time, money, and headaches.

But, if you're still with me, I thank you and applaud you. I'll reveal everything you need to know, step-by-step.

And there's no better time to start than now!

CHAPTER 5: DEFINE YOUR TARGET AUDIENCE

In order to craft a proper cold email, you need to know with whom you're speaking. Your chances of success go up geometrically when your message is tailored specifically to an exact person, instead of some faceless blob of humanity.

I realize that you might be excited to put this plan into action. You might be thinking that you can get away with sending a template and get your inbox to light up. Be advised that this step is as critical as any. You'll see exactly why in later chapters, so this step is foundational.

When it comes time to craft your message, your tone and word selection will vary depending on the audience. For example, the email I send to a 60-year-old cosmetic dentist would be different than one I would send to a 27-year-old plumber, even if the overall message is the same.

You may already be familiar with the process of creating your ideal customer's avatar. Basically, it's the process of identifying the demographics and psychographics of the ideal person that you want to work with. Once you've identified this person, down to their name, age, gender, occupation, car, house, family, and even shoe color, you then craft every message as if you are speaking directly to that avatar. By doing so, you attract the exact type of person you want to have as a client and you repel the people whom you don't want as a client.

Here is an example of an avatar:

Suzanne Hayes is a 38-year-old female. She is an attorney with a solo practice. She works out of her house but will visit clients or have lunch meetings when necessary. She is about 5'4", 130 lbs, brown hair, brown eyes, and wears glasses. When she is working at home, she is in relaxed, casual attire with her hair up in a ponytail. When she is in court or meets with clients, she wears a dark, conservative business suit with a minimum of jewelry.

Suzanne is married with 2 kids. She owns a home in the suburbs and drives a black BMW 3 Series. She loves to take brisk walks regularly, takes her kids to soccer practice every other night, and runs the occasional 5k race. In the evenings, she likes to relax at home with a good mystery novel and a glass of red wine. Her husband works as a supply chain manager. When she's not with her family, Suzanne likes to go to Starbucks with her girlfriends. When she goes on vacation, she prefers to go to the beach, but can also be found touring big cities.

Suzanne makes net $125k per year in her practice. She already has some clients and could use more, but she wants to maintain a good work/life balance. She'll work after hours more often than not to get things done. She is fairly tech savvy, and she can put up a basic website and install WordPress, but she hates doing it. She has tried marketing on her own, including SEO, AdWords, and a Facebook page, but she hasn't gotten any real results.

She is frustrated about the lack of results from her advertising and marketing efforts. She is frustrated about having to work more hours that eat in to her work/life balance. She is frustrated that she has to ask her husband for help with sending out direct mailers because she's too busy to do it herself.

She is kept up at night wondering what might happen if more attorneys come into her territory and start picking off her clients. She worries about how sites like legalzoom.com will affect her practice. She fears that she'll be left behind because other attorneys have better websites than she does.

Although she loves practicing law, she feels she has a higher calling. Suzanne dreams of being an author and publishing a book. She dreams of being asked to speak at legal conferences. She also dreams of making enough money to leave her law practice behind and spend more time with her family.

Given what we know about Suzanne, do you think you'd be able to write an effective message that she'd respond to if she were on the other end of your email?

How would you be able to formulate an avatar like Suzanne yourself? There are a lot of ways to figure it out. If you already have clients or buyers, create a composite of the perfect person who purchased your product based on what you know about your list. If not, you can research your target market on Facebook, LinkedIn, forums, blogs, and magazine media kits. Create a composite based on what you find. Or it could be someone you know personally or professionally. And you don't have to create just one.

Killer Strategy: Top 100

The late Chet Holmes, one of the greatest sales experts of our era, talked about the "Dream 100" strategy. This is when you select 100 businesses that you would absolutely be thrilled to work with. Then, when you prospect, you focus all of your energy and resources into chasing this Dream 100 until you sign up as many of them as possible. All of your emails, direct mail, calls, etc. go to these 100, and you're not contacting anyone outside of it. By doing so, you ensure that you're only working with those you find appealing to work with, and there will be enough of them that sign up to sustain your business for a long time.

This is a great strategy to pursue for cold emailing, with a twist. Instead of the Dream 100 companies you'd like to work with, you select a Top 100 list of companies in the same niche that you'd like to work with. You gain tremendous leverage when you work within the same niche, and it will save you a ton of time, increase your efficiency, and get better overall results. How? Imagine you have compiled a list of 100 Suzannes. How effective do you think your campaign might be? Do you think coming up with that avatar was a valuable exercise?

Of course, you're not limited to just 100, but the idea is to tightly focus so that the group you select is as closely aligned with your avatar as possible. The bottom line is to find COMMONALITY among everyone you're going to approach.

Need help with growing your offline marketing business?

Visit TrajectoryChange.com today!

CHAPTER 6: COMPILING PROSPECTS

The next question is how do I find the email addresses of those people I want to email?

Google. There are some slick queries you can run on Google to find prospects. For example, if I wanted to find plumbers in Phoenix, you can use this query:

```
gmail.com | comcast.net | hotmail.com
| yahoo.com site:manta.com plumbers
phoenix, az
```

This query locates Gmail, Comcast, Hotmail, and Yahoo accounts in Manta.com for plumbers in Phoenix. Manta usually also has the contact names of the businesses they list.

LinkedIn. Obviously a great source of prospects is the world's top business social network. You can use a similar query as above to find emails in LinkedIn profiles.

Scraping software. There are many programs available on the market that will enable you to scrape certain directories or sites to mine data. These programs vary in effectiveness. Some scrapers are unable to locate emails. Obviously, you will want to avoid any application that does not scrape emails. The program that I use is a program called YellaBot. This program scrapes the Yellow Pages/yp.com. Many local businesses can be found there, whether or not they pay for actual advertising.

Outsourcers. Paying an outsourcer is an extremely effective and reliable way to get leads to email. There are VAs who specialize in data collection. They have their own ways of gathering data, and they will typically tell you which sites they specialize in. They might specialize in LinkedIn, Manta, YP, Google Places, or they may have their own bots that can be programmed to scrape any collection of sites. Expect to pay anywhere from $3 to $10 or more per hour.

Some popular sites to find these vendors include odesk.com, freelancer.com or elance.com. I personally prefer elance.com. One of the best hires I've made was from elance, paying a data compiler from Bangladesh $3 per hour to find leads from different sites. In an 8-hour day, he found me up to 1200 leads, complete with contact name, email, phone number, address, and URL. That amounts to about $0.02 per lead, which is outstanding, considering that leads with this type of information can cost up to a dollar or more.

Another advantage of using a VA is that they can remove duplicates, dummy emails, or obviously irrelevant emails. This is important because if you email to bad addresses, your bounce rate goes up. The higher your bounce rate, the lower your reputation will be with your email provider (Gmail in our case), increasing your chances of being labeled as a spammer and being shut down altogether.

Business databases. Many sources on the web sell access to business databases. These include infofree. com and infousa.com. These are compiled directories that list millions of businesses across the US. You can get an account on infofree.com for about $70 per month, and it allows you to search all kinds of business databases. They have a database specifically for business owners with emails.

The drawback with infofree.com is that they only allow you to export 500 names per month. After those 500 names, they will charge you $0.05 for each additional name you export. This may not be a problem depending on your needs. If you only need the 500 emails, or you're willing to pay for the rest, then it will be the most complete data you will get for prospecting.

Using one or more of these techniques, compile a list of your Top 100. However, your research isn't done.

This next step is what will separate you from your competition, make your message stand out over the rest, demonstrate your worthiness as a business partner, increase your response rates, reduce your complaints, almost guarantee you won't end up in the spam box, and, ultimately, close deals. With so many benefits, it would make sense to follow, wouldn't it?

The next step in the lead-gathering process is to find noteworthy information on each prospect. Finding their Facebook page, Twitter feed, LinkedIn profile, or blog/article page, you will need to find something noteworthy that they said or did. You should also try to locate any news articles, events, write-ups, reviews, awards, or anything else you can reference.

For example, let's say your prospect is a plumber who was just featured in some publication called the County Journal, and they were named among the County's Best Plumbers.

There are two ways we will use this information.

The first is to use the information in the subject line. If you get this step right, you'll never again have to worry about trying to come up with the perfect subject line. For example:

```
"I saw your County Journal award"
```

The business owner would really be pretty crazy NOT to open that email.

The second way we'll use this information is what we call "the Hook" in our method. The Hook is how we get the prospect's guard down to be more receptive to the message. Typically, we'll use the Hook as the introduction or first sentence in our cold email. For example:

"Hello Frank,

I read about you recently being named one of the Top Plumbers in the County by County Journal Magazine. That's great news—congrats!"

That's about as powerful an opening line as you could ever get. You've stroked the owner's ego, and now he's invested in reading further into the email. Contrast this with something like:

"Hello Frank,

Our company can get you ranked on the first page of Google, guaranteed!"

All of us get this email, usually in our spam box, and we just chuckle at it and move on. Guess what? Your prospect is doing the same thing.

What if you can't find any noteworthy event for them? In that case, check their website or blog. You can reference something simple, such as:

"I read your article about unclogging bathtub drains. I did exactly what you said and it worked like a charm, so thank you for the valuable advice!"

Again, this is an opener that is very non-threatening, and you could easily transition this into a pitch. Of course, it helps if you actually did read their material and made a real connection with it, but it's not absolutely necessary.

Take the time to research a little about your prospect, even if it's as simple as a blog post. The time you invest up front will pay tremendous dividends in your campaign, and will clearly define you as potentially valuable to their business, not just a spammer.

Once you're done with research and lead gathering, organize everything into a spreadsheet. This will allow you to quickly execute the sending of the messages. This will also become important when you scale and automate.

CHAPTER 7: CRAFTING THE MESSAGE

Crafting a cold email is different from crafting an autoresponder message or a broadcast message. Remember that you're trying to introduce yourself to someone who doesn't know you exist. You're not trying to sell anything in that first contact.

Remember also the mindset of someone who is on the receiving end of a cold email. It's a busy business owner, or possibly a gatekeeper. He's not online 24/7 because he's actually running his business. When he gets around to checking his email, he has dozens of unread messages. Some will be from prospects asking about a quote or an appointment. Some will be from current customers who have some kind of issue. Some will be from random people who have random questions about his line of work. Some will be from friends and family. The rest are marketing/sales messages and spam.

When he scans through the inbox, which ones are going to be deleted right away? Those he deems to be spam or salesy. Which ones are going to be opened? Those he deems require his attention. If he detects your email is even the slightest bit salesy, he is conditioned, almost instinctively, to reject it off-hand. According to ExactTarget, a person takes only 2.7 seconds to decide whether to read, delete, or forward an email. With an itchy trigger finger on the delete button, it's imperative you cut through the noise and get his attention in a positive way.

For the purposes of cold emailing, you must forget everything you know about autoresponders, broadcast messages, and sales letter copywriting.

Your one and only objective with a cold email is to get a response — whether it be a reply, a phone call, or a click. Your objective is NOT to get a sale.

If you did your homework in the previous chapter, you will have half the message crafted already.

SUBJECT LINES

The subject line is the only way you will get through the door with your prospect. It has to be compelling enough, or pique enough curiosity or interest, that the prospect wants to read what's inside.

The first rule of subject lines is: No Headlines! As marketers and copywriters, we know that the purpose of the headline is to get the prospect to read the rest of the copy. For emailing, however, it doesn't work, and could get your message labeled as spam. "Finally!

An easy step-by-step method to capture leprechauns without using garlic" might sell your infoproduct, but it won't sell an open to your email.

The subject must be congruent with the rest of the message. A confused mind says "No." If there is too much disconnection between your subject line and the body of the email, confusion is inevitable. Don't use a subject line of "Your website is down" and then talk about how you admired his recent write-up in the newspaper.

If possible, make it specific. If your prospect was featured in the Wall Street Journal seven days ago, a subject line of "About your Wall Street Journal article last week" will virtually guarantee an open. Something that includes the company name also does well, as does including the owner's name. Note that the bigger the company, the less important the name becomes and the more important the company name becomes.

Ask a question. When confronted with a question, human nature practically demands an answer. A subject line containing a question will get your prospect to answer it in his head, which helps to lead him into opening the message. It doesn't have to be complicated. It can be something as simple as "Quick question?"

Split-test

Always split-test subject lines. Your goal is to always aim for the highest possible open rate, while also aiming for the highest possible CTA (call to action) rate, whether that be a phone call, reply, or click-through. The open rate is your 'traffic', and the CTA rate is your 'conversion'. Different combinations of subject lines and body copy will result in different open rates and CTAs.

To split test subject lines, use the same body copy for 2 or 3 different subjects. Send each subject line to 100 prospects a piece. Measure your statistics and see which combination of subject and body provided the best results. Then take the winning subject line and use the same one with 2 or 3 different body messages. Rinse and repeat constantly.

MESSAGE BODY

The 'meat' of your message, this is where you tell the prospect what you want from him. Obvious, right? However, it's not as easy as throwing something together mindlessly. There are many things that can go wrong here, to the point where you can get your account shut down. Follow the guidelines below to make sure you're not only safe, but that your message is received positively by your prospect.

An effective cold email message includes the following elements:

1. Hook

2. Value Proposition

3. Call to Action

Let's look at each of these in more depth.

Hook

Personalizing your message is the secret sauce that's going to make you stand out from every other message and compel your prospect to read and consider your offer. By personalizing, I don't mean just sticking his name in the salutation, although that is important as well.

When the recipient reads your message, there should be no doubt in his mind that the message was written specifically for him and only him. The very first line in your email has to show him that you're worth his time. Remember the research in Step 2? This is where it pays off.

If you found a blog post, news item, or other content written by your prospect, mention it. If what you found happens to be relevant to what you might offer, all the better. For example, your prospect might have said something on Facebook about how frustrated he is that he's not getting enough calls. He practically invited you to take his money!

If you cannot find any meaningful Hook, at the very least you should mention his name or company name. If he gets even a sniff that it might have been a mass-blasted email, it's over for that particular prospect.

VALUE PROPOSITION

What can you do for your prospect? Here you must state the reason why they should care about your message. It must be tailored to the prospect and his self-interest. This is not the time to be telling them your life story. As online marketers, this is where our training makes us want to dazzle our prospect with our sales-speak. RESIST THE TEMPTATION TO DO IT! This is not the time to show them our mastery of the Copywriting Ninja Explosion Machine course we just bought. Keep it simple, brief, straightforward, and benefit-driven. No hype. For example:

"I'm reaching out because I helped ABC Plumbing in Scottsdale increase their successful bids by 36%, which turned into $6200 in additional monthly revenue, and I'm sure I can do the same for you."

If you did your research and avatar-building correctly, you should be able to identify some kind of pain point for your prospect. Making your value proposition based on your prospect's pain points will get the most attention and response.

The value proposition is also where you can build your

credibility and social proof. If you have other clients that you've gotten results for, mention it here. If you have anything noteworthy online yourself, include it here. Sometimes, even an industry statistic might work. The key is to focus on the outcome you can bring for your prospect. He's not interested in you; he's interested in what he can gain. Keep it conversational, and not like a data sheet or catalog listing for your product or service. Remember, he doesn't know you and he's never heard of you. What would you say to help convince him that you're not trying to scam him?

CALL TO ACTION

What would you like your prospect to do? Are you looking to have him call you for a consultation? Are you looking to fill a seat in a webinar? This is where you ask them directly to perform that action. Again, it should be brief and straightforward. Limit your message to just ONE call to action. The tendency for the copywriter in us is to make the sale now. Don't do it. For a cold email to be effective, it has to move the prospect along your sales cycle in a non-threatening way, one step at a time. For example:

```
"I'm sure we can do the same for you. Do
you have 15 minutes on your calendar for
a quick chat?"
```

A reply to your email would be the least threatening and most successful call to action. It's easy for the prospect to hit reply, type a quick note, and send it, and they don't have to deal with committing to any specific action. In most cases, asking for a few minutes of time will work best. Anything more than 15 minutes is too big of an ask for the first contact.

A phone call would require a little more commitment on his part, but it's still an acceptable call to action. In fact, it may help your credibility, as having a local phone number would show that you are legitimate and not trying to hide behind an email or website.

A click-through is the least successful call to action. These days, everyone is wary of clicking on links in emails, especially from unknown senders, because of viruses or other cyber threats. There are a couple of ways around this, as you'll see below. However, know that your click-through rate will be much lower than, for example, an autoresponder campaign. That said, if you have a strong landing page with a high-converting call to action on it, the few clicks you do get might be more targeted.

If you are asking for a click, use anchor text instead of telling the prospect to Click Here. If you're sending text emails instead of HTML and can't use anchor text, then leave a naked URL. However, do not use link shorteners like bit.ly. Use a non-threatening domain name that redirects to your desired landing page. Better yet, use Facebook, LinkedIn, or some other authority link that people trust. A YouTube link will embed the video in Gmail, and it's worth split-testing.

Do NOT send any attachments!

Signature

In most cases, a simple closing will suffice:

`"Thanks,`

`Bryce"`

It's non-threatening and more personal. However, you can split-test this to see if you can sneak in an additional action.

For example, you can close your email with a URL under your name. People who are curious about your message will naturally click on your URL to do more research on you. You can lead them to a video sales letter, squeeze page or webinar sign-up form.

Another tactic I've used successfully is to add a salesy line to the signature. I've said all along to avoid salesy messages, but most people don't flinch when there's something self-promotional in the signature line. For example:

`"Thanks,`

`Bryce Jones`

`123 Main St`

Anytown, USA 12345

(555) 555-5555

Free video reveals top 3 ways to get new customers by tomorrow. Watch it now ==> www.myvideo.me"

The effectiveness will depend on your market, so test it.

PUTTING IT TOGETHER

In general, your emails will have the following structure:

[NAME]

[HOOK]

[VALUE PROPOSITION]

[CALL TO ACTION]

[SIGNATURE]

LENGTH

In the cold emailing world, less is more. You should keep the entire message to no more than 5 sentences; if you can convey your message in as little as 3 sentences, this is even better. Your prospects, who have never heard of you and don't trust you, will not give your email the time of day if they find an essay. Again, you must resist the marketer's temptation of the long-form sales letter.

Don'ts

Don't be wimpy.

Don't apologize for interrupting them. It puts you in a position of weakness and subservience.

Don't use corporate-speak.

Don't send the same message to more than one person. In other words, don't CC: anyone. If you must email two people in the same organization, send separate, and personally-crafted, messages.

Don't thank them for their time or consideration.

Don't babble on or state the obvious. Convey your point in as few words as possible.

Don't be pushy.

Don't send an attachment. I've said it before. It's worth mentioning again.

Don't confuse them with multiple calls to action or mixed messages. Stick with one objective.

Don't dress up your emails with any fancy templates or graphics. You're not sending a newsletter.

When you craft your message, do so in a Word document separate from your leads spreadsheet. This will serve as your template when you start sending out multiple messages. Also keep separate versions of your template in separate documents.

CHAPTER 8: SENDING THE MESSAGE

You have your ideal avatar. You've compiled your list. You crafted the perfect email. Now it's time to get it into the inbox of your prospect. But before you load up your message and click Send, there are a few things to heed.

Again, consider your avatar and what you think he or she would be most receptive to. It might be something informal, or you may need to project more of a professional image.

Either way, the best mail platform for our purposes is brought to you by Google. Using Google services will help your inboxing, is easy to set up, and can scale. We'll go over more about this later.

For an informal approach, a Gmail account will do just fine. Especially for the blue collar trades such as plumbing or HVAC, or for freelancers and creative types, a simple Gmail email can come across as less threatening than a slick custom domain email address. Besides, many of these businesses use free email accounts as well.

When using a Gmail account, I highly recommend that you do NOT use your own personal Gmail account for cold emailing purposes. You should establish a new one specifically for cold emailing. Ideally, you should have a separate Gmail account that has been aged with normal usage. If not, you'll need to 'warm up' the account.

Warming up an account means establishing a pattern of normal usage for a new account. In other words, after creating a new account, use it to send and receive regular emails—email your friends, other marketers, customer service reps, etc. Don't start off using it to blast the same email to cold prospects. Google will detect it and flag your account as a spammer, which affects deliverability and inboxing rates.

Warm up the account for at least 1 week. Yes, I realize that you can't wait a week to start sending emails, but this step is very important. This is the foundation of your emailing house. If you start sending cold emails without warming up the account, you're on a foundation of sand. You'll end up wasting more time later trying to recover from a flagged account than if you did it correctly to begin with.

Also, if you do create a new Gmail account, don't create a handle that is inappropriate or cutesy. Use some variation of your name, perhaps appended with a number, or use your company name. However, with reference to my earlier point about being less threatening, if your handle is MoreProfitsMarketing@gmail.com or something similar, your message will never see the light of day. Keep it low-key and not overtly salesy.

If you need a more formal and professional approach, you can still leverage the Google machine to help your cold emailing efforts. Sign up for a Google Apps account, which allows you to use the Gmail engine with your own custom domain name. You can either use one of your existing domains to attach to a Google Apps account, or you can purchase a domain dedicated to cold emailing. My advice is to create a dedicated domain for emailing. Why? If you use an existing domain and you've already been using it for regular email correspondence, you will need to change the MX records on your host server, and this could pose a problem, especially if you have multiple mailboxes or aliases. Also, if you trip up and get flagged as a spammer, it's easy to throw away a new, dedicated domain over your existing main business domain.

If you create a new domain and Google Apps account for emailing, the same rules apply for warming up an account. The same rules also apply for choosing a domain. Choose something non-threatening such as XYZresources.com. Try to avoid overtly salesy domains like IncreasedClientsMarketing.com.

Now that you have your dedicated emailing account set up and warmed up, it's time to fire away. You already know how to send an email, so just go for it, sending one at a time for as many prospects as you have on your list.

SPAM TIPS

Warming up your account properly will go a long way towards keeping your emails out of the spam box. The second way to inbox more often is to just follow the email crafting techniques we went over. That said, there are a lot of trigger words that will trip a spam filter. You can find lists of these with a quick Google search. Some big ones to avoid are:

- Click here
- No obligation
- Online marketing
- Search engine
- Double your income

If you've been following the advice laid out in this guide, you should not have a problem with spam filters. Nonetheless, still avoid any big trigger words.

CHAPTER 9: FOLLOWING UP

Your job is not done when you send the email. You must monitor your inbox for any responses. It doesn't matter what your actual call to action is. You will get replies.

However, the majority of your emails will not get a response. Most marketers will end their pursuit here. With cold emailing, that is a huge mistake. Many of your results will come from continuing to email those who don't respond. Too many times, that first email will be ignored for one reason or another, but when you send a follow-up it gets a little more attention.

Why is this so important? In sales, 84% of the TOP salespeople (those who hit their quotas 100% of the time) have a defined multi-touch strategy that includes 4-8 follow-ups. There's also an adage that it takes at least 7 contacts with a person before he buys. Either way, follow-ups are integral to the sales process. You are leaving money on the table when you don't follow up.

So, after the first email is sent, wait a day or two then send another message to everyone who did not respond to the first email. After another day or two, send another email to those who did not respond to either of the first two emails, and so on.

With a follow-up sequence, you can take a campaign with a low initial open rate and boost it significantly.

This is what is going to separate you from every other offline marketer. This is what will get you that new client more often. This is what will put more money in your pocket.

Types of responses

If the prospect responds, you should be satisfied with the fact that your message reached the inbox and was opened. You may get any number of responses, but typically, you will get:

- "Not interested/take me off your list."

- Something more threatening than "not interested."

- "I've forwarded this message to the appropriate person."

- Out of office or other auto-reply.

- A question about your offer.

- An interested response that will require a response in kind from you.

If the response is positive, then you've done your job, and you should continue the conversation to move them closer to your desired ultimate outcome for the prospect. If the response is negative, that's fine as well, because you no longer need to waste any more time on them. If you get an out of office message, pay attention to when they will return and follow up with them then.

Of course, not every message you send will be delivered. You may get a bounce-back from a bad email or an undeliverable notification due to spam. It's important to read these messages to make sure that you're not being flagged for spam. If your emails are being blocked because of spam, you may need to change your message.

How long should you wait before following up?

A Fibonacci sequence works well in spacing out follow-ups, especially if you're only going to follow up a few times. The sequence is as follows: 0, 1, 1, 2, 3, 5, 8, 13, 21, 34, 55, 89, 144, etc.

Day zero is your first message then you should follow up the next day, the day after that, 2 days after that, etc.

Ultimately, it's up to you to find a sequence that works well in your market. You'll have to monitor the responses and statistics to discover what your market will respond to best.

How many follow-ups do you send?

Send as many as you feel comfortable sending. Many

stop at the 4th message (3rd follow-up). Some continue to 8 or 10. And there are the hardy few who send follow-ups until they make the sale or are told to flip off. I have found that 5 follow-ups (6 total messages) works pretty well without annoying the hell out of the prospect. Again, you will need to find what works for you. You just never know if one more email might have made the sale.

What do you say in your follow-up?

Keep it very simple. In the first follow-up, it's just a gentle reminder about the first message, and repeating your value proposition. There's no need to do any extra or agitate the reader with a sales message.

The subject line should be the "RE: [original subject line]"

For the rest of the body, you can quote the original message along with a reminder, such as:

"Hi, [name], I just wanted to make sure that my email below didn't fall through the cracks. Let me know what you think when you have a chance. Thanks."

The second follow-up is more of the same:

"Hey, just checking in again to see what you thought about the message I sent. Let me know. Thanks."

Every subsequent follow-up needs to vary the message. You can change the value proposition completely, you can ask a question, or use any other number of approaches.

At some point, you'll probably send a final message before you write off the lead as cold. Here you can be a little more daring, maybe a little humorous, or redirect the conversation entirely.

For example:

"Hey, haven't heard from you. I just realized that I could be barking up the wrong tree. Is there anyone else I should be talking to about this? Thanks."

If the prospect just really isn't responding, you might end with something like this:

"I've attempted to reach you, but have had no success. Either you've been eaten by alligators or you're just plain swamped.

If you have been eaten by alligators, my deepest sympathy goes out to your family members.

If you're still alive, one of the following is more likely to have happened. Pick one response and let me know what my next step should be:

_____ Yes, I've been eaten by alligators. Please send flowers.

_____ No, I haven't been eaten by alligators, but you may wish I had been because I have decided I have no interest in someone helping my business. Sorry, you're sunk. (Thanks for the frank honesty. I can handle it.)

_____ Yes, I have some interest in hearing what you learned from talking to and I'm happy to talk about how to improve my business, but here are my challenges: ....

_____ Yes, it would be great to talk to like-minded people and see what good can come out of it. Call me to set a time to discuss properly.

_____ I'm not the right person, please contact ....

_____ Other: ...."

Jeremy Chatelaine, a SaaS founder, used this exact message and got a 100% response rate.

When you craft your follow-up messages, you can put them in the same document as your main template. Keep entire sequences together on the same document.

If you have multiple templates for multiple niches, for example, have a separate follow-up sequence for each template.

Don't forget that, while you're sending follow-ups, you can continue to send emails for your other campaigns. As you get deeper into cold emailing, your days will be spent sending initial emails, sending follow-ups, and responding to replies.

Need help with growing your offline marketing business?

Visit TrajectoryChange.com today!

CHAPTER 10: ADVANCED TACTIC: SCALING – THE SECRET SAUCE!

Now that you know the fundamentals of cold emailing, it's time we discuss scaling and automation.

First, a warning. Cold emailing on a mass scale does NOT mean engaging in spam! When you send cold emails on a larger scale than one at a time, you start to teeter in the direction of spamming, and we want to avoid that at all costs. If your desire is to blast as many emails as possible to as many people as possible and ignore the fundamentals of cold emailing, that is beyond the realm of what I'm teaching. You can learn more from Nigerian princes selling boner pills with Russian brides at low mortgage rates than from me.

Another warning. The bigger you scale and automate, the less effective your emails become. Note that I didn't say INeffective, because it can still work really well, and what you sacrifice in statistics you can make up for in speed and volume. But that is if, and only if, you continue to follow the fundamentals.

All that said, if you want to learn how to scale and automate your cold emailing efforts, let's move forward.

OUTSOURCING

One of the better ways to scale your emailing efforts is to hire an outsourcer or VA (Virtual Assistant). He or she can go through the entire cold emailing training and do the research, lead compiling, customization, and sending of emails and follow-ups manually on your behalf. Using the right VA, you lose very little, if any, of the effect of sending emails yourself. More emails will go out daily because the VA can just send emails all day long, every day of the week.

Additionally, you don't have to stop at one VA. You can hire as many as you want to send out as many emails as you want. In Step 4, we discussed warming up a Gmail or Google Apps account. Before you scale to multiple outsourcers, you need to make sure that the email account they're using is fully warmed up. Fortunately, you can get them to warm it up for you.

There is a big drawback to outsourcing, however.

It can get very expensive very quickly, both financially and in terms of time spent. You can pay an outsourcer anywhere from $400 to $1000 per month or more. You also have to train them and make sure they do everything correctly. And that is assuming you found a good one to start. You might go through several of them before you settle on one who can handle your requirements. Then, if you decide to hire more than one, you multiply the expense. But, if your ROI can support it, this might not be an issue.

Yet Another Mail Merge

Here is where using Google for emailing starts to pay off. There is a nifty Chrome add-on called Yet Another Mail Merge that automates sending emails. Much like the mail merge functionality in a word processor, or the variable tags in autoresponder programs, this add-on replaces variables in a document with values you set.

For example, if you have a spreadsheet that contains the first name, last name, and URL of a business owner, you can use the variable <<FirstName>> in your email template to automatically add the first name to the email. It will then send the email for you.

It's pretty easy to set up, and it enables you to send hundreds of emails at a time. All you need is a Gmail account, a Google Sheets spreadsheet, and the Chrome browser with the add-on. If you're so inclined, you can apply this to multiple warmed-up email accounts, enabling you to potentially send thousands of emails per day.

One disadvantage of using this type of 'mail merge' automation is that you start to lose a little of the effectiveness of your message. In order to send hundreds of emails in a day, you will end up sacrificing the personalization of your message. It then becomes more like a broadcast message than a personal cold email.

There is a great way to mitigate the personalization loss, however. Remember when we discussed going after one particular niche at a time? This is where that preparation pays off. If you're targeting chiropractors, for example, your template can include a sentence such as "We work with <<BUSINESS TYPE>> like yours to increase your client acquisition by 20%, just like we did for Dr. Williams in Phoenix." In your spreadsheet, you can add a column for BUSINESS TYPE and populate it with 'chiropractors' for all of the leads. It's not quite the same as the Hook we discussed in Step 3, but these are the types of compromises you'll need to make in order to scale and automate, and it at least maintains some type of personalization.

If you want to keep the original spirit of the personalization aspect of your messaging, you can add a variable in your template called <<CONNECTION>>. Then, in your spreadsheet, you would have a column for CONNECTION, and you would populate each cell with the personalization you found for each individual prospect. This additional step, although a little more time consuming and tedious, maintains the power of a manual cold email in respect to speed and scale.

Another disadvantage is that it does not automate follow-ups. You will need to monitor your inboxes and respond to the people who replied to you. You will then need to manually find who did not respond and send them a follow-up. Of course, you can semi-automate the follow-up with this add-on, but there is a lot of manual spreadsheet manipulation to deal with.

All things considered, this is a slick way to increase your volume exponentially, reduce the time it takes to send a high volume of emails, and, best of all, it's completely free.

MY SECRET WEAPON

This next method is the one I personally use and thrive with. Although it is being used in the Silicon Valley startup world fairly regularly, it is largely unknown in the Internet Marketing world. It is my secret weapon.

What if there was a way to combine the power and functionality of your favorite autoresponder with the principles of cold emailing, while still using your Gmail or Google Apps account so that it looks like it was sent by you personally, even if it wasn't, AND automates the follow-up process for you?

It does exist! It's called QuickMail.

QuickMail is a SaaS program that automates the cold emailing process. You load up a template, fill it with variables, load up your spreadsheet, and schedule the email to be sent. You can do multiple campaigns, so if you have multiple niches you can set a campaign for each one. It allows you to split test emails automatically. It keeps all of your statistics, including open rate, response rate, and click-through rate. It has real-time notifications to let you know the very moment an open or click occurs, which means that you can immediately follow up with a phone call while the lead is hot. Lastly, it automatically sends follow-up messages if a prospect does not open your email, and those who do reply are automatically removed from the follow-up sequence. It has even more features than that, but, for our purposes, this is a pretty comprehensive feature set.

You might be asking how this differs from an autoresponder.

There are definitely many similarities. Both QuickMail and autoresponders are template-based, can schedule outbound emails, can automate a follow-up sequence, can split-test, and can keep statistics among other things. However, some differences include:

QuickMail is designed for outbound cold emailing campaigns because it sends email directly from your Google account instead of third-party servers. When email is sent through a third-party server, which includes autoresponders, it is meant for bulk sending. The recipient will read the email and find a tagline somewhere in the message that says it was "sent via [some code or URL]." That's a dead giveaway that the message was not sent personally.

QuickMail is not an opt-in system. A prospect cannot fill in an opt-in form to be added to QuickMail. It is designed to send emails to prospects with whom you have no previous relationship, so you're not expected to have gathered them in any particular manner. Conversely, autoresponders only work on opt-in. You can import leads into an autoresponder, but, in most cases, they need to confirm being added.

Autoresponders are designed to send thousands of emails per day. QuickMail is designed to send hundreds of emails per day, although the software has no technical limit. You are only limited by the number of emails Google allows you to send. That is a good thing, because your prospects don't know you and did not request anything from you.

Autoresponders are designed to send follow-ups indefinitely, and can move subscribers to different lists and campaigns depending on an action that the subscriber took. The only follow-up sequence that QuickMail does is to send automatic replies to prospects who did not reply to your first message. It will actually continue to send as many follow-ups as you configure it to send, or until everyone on your list responds, whichever comes first. Once a lead responds, they are removed from follow-up sequences completely. This is one of the most powerful money-making features of QuickMail. Automating the tedium of sending follow-ups is a huge timesaver. You can just allow QuickMail to continue to follow up for you, which will get your overall open rates above the 50% mark or higher.

You can use QuickMail in conjunction with an autoresponder.

Use the same tips for personalization outlined in the Yet Another Mail Merge section to maximize results.

QuickMail costs $37 per month for the standard account and $67 for the Pro account. If you're bootstrapping, you probably don't need the Pro account to start, as the standard has all of the basic functionality that you'll need. But if you can get the Pro, it includes real-time notifications,

As icing on the cake, QuickMail's founder, Jeremy Chastelaine, is a wonderful guy. He's very sharp, responsive, and cares about every single one of his customers. He also has a great blog that spotlights many of the successes that people experience using his system.

Check out QuickMail at www.quickmail.io.

For the ultimate automatic prospecting solution, combine outsourcing with QuickMail. Have your VA run and monitor your QuickMail campaigns. If you trust him to respond then he can respond on your behalf to those who reply to you.

With a tool as powerful as QuickMail at your disposal, the temptation will be to maximize send limits and blast out as many messages as you can get away with.

DO NOT DO IT!

There are several reasons why you shouldn't:

1. Doing so will put you squarely in spam territory.

2. You will find that the more campaigns and emails you send, the more responses you're going to get. Each positive response is an interested prospect raising his hand to learn more about your offer. Each one deserves your full attention. When you automate, it won't be long before you'll be overwhelmed with responses. Keep your prospecting machine going at the 'sweet spot' where you're sending enough messages to fill your pipeline while being able to service every response you get.

3. You will get your Gmail and Google Apps accounts shut down. I recommend sending no more than 200 emails per day, per Gmail account. That is well below Google's send limit, and it will keep you largely under the radar.

4. You need to iterate your emails. In other words, every 100-200 messages you'll want to see what's working and what's not working, and then make changes. Then

repeat after the next 100-200 messages, and so on. By doing so, you increase your response rates and craft a message that really resonates with your audience. Use QuickMail's split-testing feature to get there even faster. You don't want to send out 2,000 emails only to find out that they weren't effective or had some kind of error, like a typo. Better that you find that out after 100 emails, and then make the change.

CHAPTER 11: ATTRACT

If you're already successfully running a Digital Marketing Agency (DMA) or other offline/local marketing business, cold emailing might be enough for you to accomplish your goals. However, if you're struggling to grow your business, are starting a new one, or want a better way to differentiate yourself and skyrocket your company's potential, the remaining chapters will explain how to accomplish that.

For those that are new to the local marketing game, I'm going to help you start a Digital Marketing Agency (DMA), in which you'll provide online services to offline businesses, such as SEO, social media management, PPC, consulting, or whatever else you want to offer. You may already have one. Or, maybe you don't want to start a DMA, but rather focus more on online marketing with this method. That's fine, too. Most of the steps are the same, and we'll go into DMA alternatives in the later chapters. Either way, we're going to change things up a bit.

As has been the dominant theme in everything I've said so far, we're going to shift our mindsets and show a different approach to what people generally go about executing.

You will position your DMA/online business as a publishing company.

Why a publishing company? Because everyone who has ever bought an offline marketing course has created marketing agencies, SEO agencies, PPC agencies, offline marketing consulting, and on and on. Here's the problem. When you approach a business saying that you're any of these things, their salesman detection system starts beeping. They know you're trying to sell them something. Their guard goes up, which is another obstacle in your way. So let's flip things around and approach them with something they want.

If you approach them as a publishing company with the intention of interviewing or featuring them in a published, physical paperback book, they will be more receptive to hear what you have to say. Being "chosen" for an interview is much more flattering than being picked out of a Google listing to be sold some product or service.

I want to go over the general strategy at a high level so that you understand how we're going to leverage your publishing company to get hot prospects and turn them into high-paying clients.

There are actually a myriad of ways to carry out the general strategy. To keep things simple in this course, we're going to focus on publishing a paperback book. You can also use this strategy with any other tactics such as videos, podcasts, whitepapers, magazines, blogs, etc. When you finish this course, feel free to adapt it as your creativity allows.

Don't worry, you're not going to have to sit at a typewriter for month on end to write a book, 99% of the content will be provided for you.

To get started with this, you'll pick a niche to target. You will then approach your prospects from that niche via cold email outreach and let them know that you want to interview them for an upcoming book you're putting on Amazon. For example, you might be targeting real estate agents. You send them a cold email, which is included in this course, letting them know that your publishing company is putting together a paperback book on how to navigate the home buying process for first-time homebuyers. You'd like to interview them and feature them in the book at no cost or obligation to them.

They will respond, either with a yes, no or asking for more information. Either way, you'll get engagement, which is what we're after.

With your correspondence, you get them interested in participating in the book project. You then send them a list of about 10 to 15 questions. The questions are frequently asked questions that a new homebuyer would ask.

They answer the questions, return them to you, and you compile (copy and paste) about 10 to 12 of the real estate agents into the book. Mind you, up to this point, you have not spent a dime on "marketing."

You then give the interviewees the opportunity to purchase the book at wholesale (don't worry, this is much easier than it sounds), so you can generate income.

You compile the book, launch it on Amazon, and show your prospects the new book in which they're featured. For additional credibility, you can launch a Kindle version and get it to become a bestseller.

Then, leveraging this book and the new relationship you have with your prospects, you upsell them any number of ways to generate income.

That's about it in a nutshell.

Don't worry, we'll go over how to execute this plan in more detail, and it's all much easier than it sounds, including publishing and printing the book. This is a high-level overview to get your creative juices flowing.

CHAPTER 12: SETUP

The first step is to come up with a name for your publishing company. Make it something generic but brandable. In other words, create a name that looks like a legitimate company and unique, but not specific to a product or service. Don't just say Social Media Experts Publishing. Try something like Buzzbuilder Publishers. And I say "generic" because we don't want to be boxed into a specific type of publisher. So avoid Mango Books or Mango News. Instead, try Mango Press or Mango Publishing Group. That will give you more flexibility in your business later on.

Register a domain for it. I use namecheap.com or godaddy.com. Make sure to find a coupon code to get your domain as cheaply as possible.

Next, you'll need a solid website host. There are hundreds to choose from, and they each offer all kinds of different packages. Don't complicate this, just pick a host with a good reputation, such as LiquidWeb, and choose a cheap package. You don't need a lot of horsepower for your site.

Then, you'll need to get your website ready to be

designed. Once you are able to access your website after you get your domain and hosting set up, install WordPress. If you have any problems with installing WordPress, or any other part of getting your website set up, hop on over to Fiverr and get it done for you for only $5.

Next, you'll need an easy page builder and funnel system to put your new publishing company site together.

My preference is InstaBuilder: http://www. totalmarketingstrategists.com/instabuilder

This program plugs into WordPress and lets you build out sites easily and quickly. You can then churn out a full-blown marketing funnel so that you can lead your prospects to a sale on autopilot.

Alternatively, you can install the WP theme of your choice. Just make sure it looks professional like a big publishing house.

Before you can start approaching potential clients, you'll need to have your website built out. Your prospects will want to see something from you, so you'll need to look legitimate. Of course, the goal here is to actually BE legitimate. This is a strategy that you can use to build a long-term, sustainable business, so it's time you conduct business as such.

This does not mean you have to build out some

elaborate web presence. A simple website with a homepage, About page, and Contact page will work. But it does need to look clean and professional.

As for the content of the site, that is completely up to you, your creativity, and what kind of publishing model you'll actually be doing. At minimum, your home page should answer the following:

- What's your company and specialty (i.e. We are a publishing company that showcases local business experts and how they can help consumers tackle their challenges)?

- Who do you serve (i.e. We work with business owners such as real estate agents, home improvement companies, and real estate investors)?

- What is your promise/mission (i.e. Our mission is to elevate the expertise and credibility of local business owners to help them stand out from their competitors and be seen as the go-to resource for their potential customers)?

The examples I gave are very broad and general. You should be more specific in what you do to help focus your efforts.

You should also have an About page to tell people about you, your expertise, more about your mission, and how you can help them. Lastly, you should have a Contact page to tell people how to get in touch with you. It can be as simple as an email submission form, or you can put your company address and phone number if you're going to communicate by phone.

If you are trained in copywriting, you can use your skills for your website. If not, basic information about what you do will suffice. The goal of the website is not really to sell your prospects. It's to show them that you have a legitimate presence and to tell them a little about you. The real selling will happen during the email exchange.

By the way, you don't need testimonials, case studies, or even samples of your work. It helps, and you can add those later, but it's not absolutely necessary when you're starting out, so don't let that stop you.

The point is, do not get hung up on making your website perfect. Good enough is good enough. I know the tendency is to keep tweaking and making everything perfect before moving on to the next step. If you do that, you will never get started. Take action now! You can always change things later.

CHAPTER 13: NICHE SELECTION

Now the fun begins!

The big question is, who, or what niche, are you going to target?

In trying to answer this question, you need to consider the following:

1. Do people purchase books written about, or authored by, your target?

2. Does your niche's target audience, whether it be businesses or consumers, seek them out?

3. Are there directories or trade associations that your target might belong to or be listed in?

4. Is your target's expertise something that people research to look for answers or solutions?

5. Is your target's service limited to a local area, or can they provide their service nationwide?

6. Do they have the willingness, ability, and the need for whatever services you'll eventually offer them?

To answer these questions, spend a little time browsing through Amazon or your local bookstore, in the non-fiction section, of course. With regard to #5, this may or may not be a roadblock. If you were writing a book, for example, you could stay with the local theme and write your city's guide to the best local providers of your target niche. The benefit to your target is that they would be featured in a local guide and potentially get some business out of it. If you wanted to write a book on a more general topic, such as a book on how to make high-value home improvements on a budget, for example, you could feature contractors from around the country. The benefit to them is that they can say they're featured in a book as one of the top experts nationwide, which would help elevate their status locally and close more sales.

Let's look at some examples of potential niches.

Home Improvement: This might include general contractors, or it might be a more specific trade, such as painters, flooring contractors, or kitchen remodeling contractors.

Book idea: How To Make High-Value Improvements To Your Home On A Budget

Finance: This can include Certified Financial Planners, accountants, insurance agents, or mortgage lenders.

Book idea: The Secret Financial Planning Tricks That

Only The Professionals Know.

Wedding: This can include wedding planners, caterers, venue operators, travel agents, or high-end wedding dress boutiques.

Book idea: How To Plan The Perfect Wedding, From Cake To Honeymoon.

As you can see, there is no limit to how creative you can get with this, and you can target a wide variety of niches.

After you decide on a target niche, you need to:

- Come up with a title or concept for your published work. The book ideas above are a good place to start brainstorming.

- Compile a list of 30 questions that you will send to your prospect to "interview" them. Run searches for your target niche and FAQs. Look at their websites, check forums, Reddit, magazines, and other books.

CHAPTER 14: PUBLISHING PROSPECTING

Using the principles outlined in Chapter 6, you can start compiling your leads, if you haven't already.

Next, you're going to reach out to your prospects to get them into your funnel.

When you're ready to get started, deploy Email 1.

```
Subject: {Niche Type} Needed

Body:

Hello {First Name},

{Publishing Company} is looking for a
{Niche Type} to interview for a {type of
work} we're publishing, called "{Title}."
There is no cost or obligation for
participating. If you're interested in
being featured in the {type of work},
please reply no later than {deadline -
2 or 3 business days from email send
date}, and I'll forward you the interview
questions.
```

Thanks,

{Your Name}

Associate Publisher

www.yourpublishingcompany.com

Here's an example of what this would look like:

Subject: Kitchen Remodeler Needed

Body:

Hello Frank,

Buzzbuilder Publishing is looking for a kitchen remodeler to interview for an Amazon Kindle book we're publishing, called "High-Value Home Improvements on a Budget." There is no cost or obligation for participating. If you're interested in being featured in the book, please reply no later than Friday, March 13, and I'll forward you the interview questions.

Thanks,

Jodi McGuire

Associate Publisher

www.yourpublishingcompany.com

If you're ready to start sending emails, go for it! The

sooner you take action; the sooner you can start to generate revenue.

Once you start sending, expect to get responses. How do you handle these?

Ideally, they will tell you that they're interested and ask for the interview questions, or ask for the next step. The next step is for you to email them the interview questions. I'll go over that template in a minute. First, let's discuss how to handle the other frequently asked questions you'll get.

One of the most common responses I get is: Can you show me samples of your work? Can I see other books you've published? Or some other variation of the same.

If you're new and don't have any type of testimonials, case studies, samples, etc., you would respond like this:

```
Hello {First Name},

Thanks for your question. We are a
startup company. However, we do have an
experienced team.

Thanks,

{Your Name}
```

Another frequently asked question is: What's the benefit? What do I get out of this?

Here's a response that quiets that down every time:

```
Hello {First Name},

The primary benefit to you is that you'll
be featured in a published paperback book
on Amazon, which instantly gives you
higher credibility and showcases your
expertise. You can use that book to show
your customers. You can also use it for
your own marketing and advertising, so
you stand out among your competitors.

Thanks,

{Your Name}
```

Sometimes people wonder why they were "chosen" for the honor of being featured in your publication. They'll often ask: How did you hear about me?

```
Hello {First Name},

We have a "scouting team" that use a variety
of resources and criteria to identify
potential candidates for interviews.
Based on what they found, they thought
you might be a good fit for this project.

Thanks,

{Your Name}
```

Lastly, people frequently ask what kind of cost there is associated with participating. They also ask if they get any royalties or some other type of compensation for participating. Here's how to respond:

```
Hello {First Name},

There is no cost or obligation for
participating. We also do not compensate
for participation. The main benefit to you
is that you'll be featured in a published
paperback book on Amazon, which instantly
gives you higher credibility and showcases
your expertise. You can use that book to
show your customers. You can also use it
for your own marketing and advertising,
so you stand out among your competitors.

Thanks,

{Your Name}
```

If their initial reply to you was any of these, you would have broken down any resistance to your offer. You'll also be establishing rapport with them, which is crucial for when you upsell to a paid service.

Their next response after this should be to let you know that they want to participate. If so, deploy Email 2, the Interview Questions template.

A couple of notes about the template:

Make sure they fill it out correctly, especially the top part titled "TERMS" to protect you from any disputes. This gives you the right to use their content however you see fit.

Earlier, I had you compile 30 questions. Choose 15 of them to send to your prospect and insert them into the template. I recommend sending the same questions to each prospect, so you have some consistency in the book.

At the bottom of the questions, you'll see a section of 3 questions that will NOT be published. This is a secret ninja tactic I use. Because they're already in a question-answering mood, it's the perfect time to hit them up with any questions you have to help figure out what their needs are. That way, you can structure your offer or training material accordingly. I included 3 questions I use, but feel free to use whatever questions that fit your specific situation.

```
- - - - - - - - - - - - - I N T E R V I E W
TEMPLATE-----------------

Hello {FIRST NAME},

Thanks for your interest in participating
in this book project!

There are two sections below. The first
section is the Terms section. Please
review prior to submitting your interview
```

answers. If you agree to the Terms, type your full name, your company name, and your position/title with your company in the fields below.

The second section is the interview questions and instructions.

The deadline to complete both sections is 5 business days.

TERMS: By submitting your answers to the interview questions contained herein, you acknowledge that all of the information you provide will become the property of {YOUR PUBLISHING COMPANY NAME}. {YOUR PUBLISHING COMPANY NAME} has the right to use the information that you submit in any book title(s) they choose to publish. You also understand and acknowledge that you are submitting this content as a means of promotion for your company and that you will not be compensated by {YOUR PUBLISHING COMPANY NAME} for providing this information, nor will you be entitled to receive any royalty payments or other compensation for the sales of any books that include the information you've submitted to {YOUR PUBLISHING COMPANY NAME}. You will not be required to compensate {YOUR

PUBLISHING COMPANY NAME} in any way for this promotion that is being provided to your company. {YOUR PUBLISHING COMPANY NAME} reserves the right to publish all, part, or none of the information that you submit. Prior to publishing any books that contain the content you've submitted, {YOUR PUBLISHING COMPANY NAME} reserves the right to edit the information that you submit for: grammatical errors, quality control issues, or for any other purpose that {YOUR PUBLISHING COMPANY NAME} deems appropriate.

By submitting the interview questions contained herein, I hereby understand and agree to the terms stated above:

FULL NAME:

COMPANY NAME:

TITLE/POSITION WITH COMPANY:

Instructions for completing the interview questions below:

Preceding the set of interview questions, you may provide information about your company, including your company name, a description of the products/services you provide, your website, your phone number, your social media profiles, and any other contact details that you'd like to include. For the interview questions themselves, however, please avoid overly promotional/commercial sounding answers. The objective of your interview answers should be to educate and inform the reader, not promote your company within the interview answers themselves. Please use the fields preceding the interview questions to share information about your company and use the interview questions as a way of educating the reader so that they will view you as a trusted authority on the subject matter. Please avoid one-word or one-sentence answers to the questions. Please try to provide as much detail as possible to each question. Providing detailed answers will further show the reader that you are knowledgeable about the subject matter.

Please tell us about your company here:

Please tell us how readers can get in contact with you here:

Please answer each interview question

directly below each question.

Question 1: {INSERT YOUR QUESTION HERE}

Question 2: {INSERT YOUR QUESTION HERE}

Question 3: {INSERT YOUR QUESTION HERE}

Question 15: {INSERT YOUR QUESTION HERE}

Questions to be answered by the {BUSINESS TYPE} about him/herself (will not be published):

What are three frustrations you have with your {BUSINESS TYPE} business?

What are three issues that keep you up at night regarding your {BUSINESS TYPE} business?

Where would you like to see yourself and your {BUSINESS TYPE} business 1 year from now?

Thanks,

{YOUR NAME}

Associate Publisher

{YOUR URL}

So now you should have everything you need to facilitate a dialog with your prospect. Of course, you will have other questions or scenarios that pop up. You will need to handle those however you see fit, it's not possible to give an answer to every possible scenario. You're running a business now, so think and act as a business owner would.

You're shooting for about 10 to 12 completed interviews. It will take you about a week to get all the interviews, sometimes longer. Keep on top of those that you sent the interview to so you can get the answers back in a reasonable enough time for you to do your thing.

When you do receive the answers, make sure to thank them for doing so. Deploy Email 3:

```
Hello {FIRST NAME},

Thank you for submitting your answers to
our interview questions.

We will be reviewing the content you've
submitted over the next few days. We
will also email you within the next five
business days if we have questions about
the content you've submitted to us, and
for any follow-up questions.

I appreciate your time in participating
in this project! I'll keep you posted on
any developments as well. If you have any
questions, please let me know.
```

Thanks,

{YOUR NAME}

Associate Publisher

{YOUR URL}

CHAPTER 15: BOOK CONSTRUCTION

While you're waiting for the interview answers to come in, you should get started on producing your book.

By the way, even though you're waiting for interview answers, you should continue to contact prospects. Any additional answers you get can be used for a second edition of your book. The more editions you have, the better your chances of securing clients from an upsell. If you've followed everything so far, you're going to be busy fielding responses to your campaigns every day.

Now would be a good time to start your book cover. If you're having trouble with prospects not wanting to be interviewed because you're new, you'll want to get the cover done as soon as possible. That way, you can show them that it's legitimate.

There are three ways you can get the cover done:

- You can do the cover yourself

- You can outsource it to Fiverr

- You can use CreateSpace's cover designer for free (we'll go over this method in the next section).

If you're doing it yourself, the best resource is DIY Book Covers (www.diybookcovers.com). They have very professional layouts for real books. I'm not talking about the cheesy 3D ebook covers that you get for Internet Marketing products (including this one, ha!). I'm talking about quality covers that are good enough to be on a bookstore bookshelf. Please don't go the route of the 3D internet marketing covers. As marketers, we've been conditioned to perceive these as quality, but 99% of them look terrible, even ones created for very high ticket courses.

Also, when you create your cover, put some kind of prominent graphic or picture on the front. This will become important later when we cover income-producing methods.

The paperback book size will be 5.5"x8.5". Keep that in mind when designing your cover. Whoever is designing the cover will also need to know how many pages your book will have in order to create the proper width of the book's spine. It's okay if it's not precise. When you go to publish the book, there are mechanisms in place to make sure your book comes out fine. Typically, 10 interview responses will yield around an 80 to 100-page book, depending on how you lay it out and what other material you might want to include in it.

As far as the insides of the book, it's as easy as filling

in the blanks. I've included a book template for you to use.

Start filling in the details of your book in the template. When you get the interview answers back, you can paste them into the template as you go.

If you're so inclined, you should also start writing the "Front Matter" of the book. These include the Foreword, Preface, and Introduction. This is optional. The vast majority of the content will be the interview answers. However, you may wish to add a more professional touch by including the Front Matter.

You don't need to write all of it. For most cases, just an Introduction will work. Just write a 500- to the 1000-word article, or have it written for you and introduce the book's contents. The rest of the book will be filled in with the interviews. If you have a personal story or connection with the subject matter of the book, also write a Preface that tells your story. This makes the work more meaningful, both for you and the interviewees, which will build even deeper rapport. For example, if you're interviewing personal trainers for your book, and you happened to lose 100 lbs with the help of one, that would be a great story to include in the Preface.

You'll find that even though you gave a deadline, you won't get some of the answers back for another week or two. As soon as you have enough interviews to fill your book, you can move forward. If not, you'll have to wait until you do.

When you have the entire template filled out, it's time to work on finishing your book. The next step is to format, proofread and edit the book. This step is important because it puts a professional polish on the book. You don't want to put something out there with typos, grammatical errors, and formatting inconsistencies. That would reflect very poorly on your "publishing company."

Here's how to approach this.

First, you need to read the whole thing for grammatical and spelling errors. If spelling and grammar aren't your strong suit, consider hiring an editor or proofreader on Fiverr. They'll make sure that the entire book, including your Front Matter, flows and reads nicely.

After having the content edited, you'll need to have the text formatted for presentation.

First, format the book so that the font is the same for the entire book. It doesn't really matter what font you use as long as it's one that you might expect to see in a book you'd see on the shelf. Times New Roman should do. Next, make sure all the regular text, such as your Front Matter and the interview answers, is the same size (12 point).

For extra polish, bold the interview questions. Also,

make sure that any headers and chapter titles are a larger size and bolded. Then, make sure everything is aligned and justified to the left. If you want to center titles and headers, do so, but do not center the regular text. Finally, insert page numbers and a Table of Contents. If this sounds like too much of a hassle for you, you can find a layout designer on Fiverr. Many do a great job and format books specifically for Kindle.

If you are using Fiverr for any of these tasks, note that not all editors will format/layout the text, and not all formatters will edit/proofread the text.

Once both editing and layout are finished, you can upload the book to CreateSpace for publishing.

CreateSpace is the self-publishing arm of Amazon. They will publish and print your book on demand, as well as list it for sale on Amazon. It's also where you will get your royalty payments for any books you've sold. Since it's a print-on-demand (POD) platform, it means that books are printed when they're sold. No need to buy a stack of thousands to store in your garage. One bonus perk, which is what makes this system possible, is that they have special pricing for you, the publisher, and they will ship your book anywhere for you.

We'll go over how to use CreateSpace a little later.

Need help with growing your offline marketing business?

Visit TrajectoryChange.com today!

CHAPTER 16: MONEY METHOD 1 – WHOLESALE

Let me ask you a question. If a publishing company approached you, interviewed you for your expertise, and published a book about it, would it not be something you'd be proud to share with friends, family, clients, and prospects?

I'm betting you would, as would many others.

Under that premise, you will offer the same courtesy to the folks that you interviewed and get paid for it!

What you'll do is calculate what it will cost for you to produce a certain number of books. Then you'll set your own "wholesale" price, which is what you'll present to the interviewees. The difference between what it costs you and what you charge is your profit. You'll then order the appropriate quantity of books and ship them directly to the client.

What's great about this is that you don't have to pay anything until the client pays you! You don't have to print any books until the client pays you.

This page on CreateSpace calculates what your cost will be: https://www.createspace.com/Products/Book/#content7

Once you have all the interview answers back, and your book constructed, you'll know how many pages your book will be. You'll need this information to calculate your cost.

You also need to know how many books you want to sell. My recommendation is to set a minimum wholesale order of 50 units. Lastly, you will need to calculate shipping. It's best to include shipping into the wholesale cost rather than charging your client for it, but that's up to you.

Here's an example scenario. Let's say your book is 100 pages, and you want to sell 50 copies, and you're covering the shipping. According to the calculator:

$2.15 per book

$107.50 for 50 copies

The shipping cost for 50 copies in the Continental US is $23 for Standard shipping.

Total cost to you is $130.50.

The $130.50 is what you will pay CreateSpace to have 50 copies of your book printed and shipped to your client.

Let's say you want to make $5 profit per book.

$2.15 + $0.46 (shipping per book) + $5.00 = $7.61 (This is your wholesale rate per book.)

$7.61 x 50 copies = $380.50 (This is what you will charge your client.)

$380.50 - $130.50 = $250.00 (This is your profit for an order of 50 books.)

It's up to you what you want to charge, so you could make even more than that, but remember to keep the cost reasonable for your client because they will be able to buy your book for retail price on Amazon. Keep your price a comfortable amount below retail. Anywhere from $3-$5 wholesale profit per book works well. Of course, if they end up buying retail instead, you'll make a royalty on that purchase, so you win either way.

Now, the $250 is for just one order of 50 books. If you have 10 interviewees in the book:

$250.00 x 10 clients = $2500.00 (This is your profit if all 10 interviewees bought 50 copies at wholesale.)

So, for sending a few emails and copying and pasting into a template, you can make up to $2,500 per book!

Remember, too, that 50 copies is the suggested minimum. They might want to order more than that, and you will give them the option to do so.

If you are diligent with your prospecting, you can get to the point where you're cranking out 1 book per week. You can do your own math as to the profit potential of that scenario.

This chart shows you what your profit potential can be per order:

Quantity for 100 page book	Your Member Price ($2.15 per book)	Shipping	Total Cost	Desired Profit ($5 per book)	Your Client Price
50	$107.50	$23.00	$130.50	$250.00	$380.50
100	$215.00	$43.00	$258.00	$500.00	$758.00
150	$322.50	$63.00	$385.50	$750.00	$1,135.50
200	$430.00	$83.00	$513.00	$1,000.00	$1,513.00
250	$537.50	$103.00	$640.50	$1,250.00	$1,890.50
300	$645.00	$123.00	$768.00	$1,500.00	$2,268.00

The "Your Client Price" column is what you will charge your clients in order to make $5 profit per book if $5 is your target. Use the calculator to adjust for your specific situation.

On your website, you'll want to set up a Member's Area that can only be accessed by your interviewees. This should be a stand-alone page that isn't linked in your website navigation. You don't want the general public stumbling on to the page; you only want your interviewees to access it.

Inside that Member's Area, set up a shopping cart page where they can place the order. There are numerous ways to accomplish this with all kinds of different applications.

I use InstaMember (www.insta-member.com) as my membership portal, and then I use Wufoo forms for the shopping cart form. Wufoo forms (www.wufoo. com) integrate with Stripe or Paypal, so you can create a form with your purchase options along with the fields to collect billing and shipping information.

On the wholesale order page, you should include:

- Book cover image
- Book description
- Wholesale pricing selection
- Order/Add to cart/Checkout button

You should also note that shipping is included in the price (if you opted to do so) and that it will take 2-3 weeks for delivery to give you a cushion to get the book published.

When you're done setting up your order page, contact your clients to give them the opportunity to make the purchase. Note that you don't even have to have your book 100% ready and complete before asking for the wholesale order.

To ask your interviewees to make a wholesale purchase, you will deploy Email 4:

```
Hi {FIRST NAME},
```

Congratulations! I'm pleased to inform you that your content has been reviewed and approved for inclusion in our book, "{BOOK TITLE}."

As you're probably aware, being featured in a book that's related to your industry can have an extremely positive influence on prospective customers who are considering doing business with you. We understand that you will likely want to share copies of this book with prospective and existing customers, as well as with your friends and family. To make it easy for you to share this book with whomever you'd like, we have extended to you the option to purchase "{BOOK TITLE}" at the same wholesale pricing that bookstores and book distributors receive.

We have created an exclusive Contributors area for you, which will allow you to access the wholesale purchasing area. Please do not share this page with others, as our wholesale pricing data is confidential. There is absolutely no obligation to make a purchase.

To log in to the Contributors area of our site, please go to:

{BOOK-SPECIFIC MEMBERS AREA LINK}

Please register on this page to access the wholesale details.

Congratulations again on being featured in "{BOOK TITLE}!" Please let me know if you have any questions.

Thanks,

{YOUR NAME}

Associate Publisher

{YOUR URL}

The email directs your client to register on your wholesale order page to place an order.

When they do place an order, you'll need to fulfill it. In CreateSpace, you'll place a Member Order. Make sure the price you're being charged is congruent with what you calculated in the Member Calculator. You'll input your information for the billing information, and you'll input the client's information for shipping. CreateSpace will send your client the books they ordered directly. Of course, you'll need the book to be finished first, which we will cover in the next chapter.

Also, when they place an order, deploy the Wholesale Thank You email:

Hi {FIRST NAME},

Thank you for placing your wholesale order for {BOOK TITLE}. Please allow 2-3 weeks for shipping.

Here are your order details:

Quantity of Books Ordered: {#}

Total Paid: {$xxx}

Shipping Address:

{SHIPPING RECIPIENT'S NAME}

{SHIPPING STREET ADDRESS}

{SHIPPING CITY, STATE, AND ZIP CODE}

If you have any questions, please let me know

Thanks again for your order! Enjoy sharing {BOOK TITLE} with your customers and prospective customers, as well as with your friends and family!

Thanks,

{YOUR NAME}

Associate Publisher

{YOUR URL}

Now, what if they don't place an order? Don't fret, because there will be many ways to generate income from your clients. We'll touch on those later. First, we have to publish your book!

Need help with growing your offline marketing business?

Visit TrajectoryChange.com today!

CHAPTER 17: PUBLISHING AND PRINTING

To set up your CreateSpace account, go to www. CreateSpace.com. If you already have an Amazon.com account that you use for your personal shopping, use that same email address for CreateSpace.

You'll receive a member ID number and dashboard.

Click the blue Add New Title button. This takes you to the Start Your New Project page.

On the Start Your New Project page, fill in the name of your book, the type of project and choose a setup method.

There are two choices:

- Guided: A step-by-step process with directions along the way.

- Expert: A streamlined single-page experience for those familiar with the process.

Click the Get Started button by your choice and move on to the next step. I recommend Guided to start, and then you can use Expert when you get the hang of it.

TITLE INFORMATION PAGE:

Fill in your book title and subtitle (if applicable). For author name, you can put your own name, a pen name, or the name of your publishing company, whichever you prefer.

There is a contributor's field. Here, you will put in the names of everyone you interviewed that will be included in the book. Put them in one at a time, and choose Interviewee as the type of contributor.

You can also put in a series name and number (if applicable) and other details.

Note: If you leave Publication Date blank, the date your book publishes on CreateSpace will be added. If you published the book previously, on Kindle for instance, or with a traditional publisher, you could fill in the original pub date if you wish.

Click Save & Continue.

ISBN:

CreateSpace says, "An ISBN (number) is required to publish and distribute a book."

They offer four options. One is free. You can use the free one if you're not inclined to pay anything, but I strongly recommend you choose Custom ISBN because this allows you to use your publishing company as the publisher on record. This costs $10. The free option makes CreateSpace the publisher, which does nothing for your branding or professionalism. Compare the options carefully because once you make your choice it cannot be changed. Choose and click Continue.

INTERIOR:

Choose:

- black & white
- white paper color
- trim size (size of your book): 5.5"x 8.5"

Then comes the "fun" part, uploading your book!

You can either hire a CreateSpace professional to do it for you, with prices starting at $349 or you can do it yourself. I recommend you do it yourself.

DO IT YOURSELF METHODS:

Upload your work as a print-ready .pdf, .doc, .docx, or .rtf file.

NOTE: Please see http://www.trajectorychange. com/createspace for templates, screenshots, and book construction guides. This chapter corresponds to images found on the website.

The thumbnails on the left show how a CreateSpace formatted template is set up. The template included with this course can be used for CreateSpace. Each pair of pages represents the front and back sides of one printed page. The left page of each pair would actually be the right-hand page in a book while the right one would be on the left (backside of right page.)

The midline in each pair represents the outside edge of the page; the left and right borders are the edge of the page that would be bound, forming the book's spine. Because more space is necessary on the bound edge, the text must be offset closer to the outside edge (the center line of each pair.) See this spacing difference in the illustration above.

There is a table of contents included in the formatted template. If you don't want one in your book, simply delete that pair of pages. You can also delete the dedication and acknowledgements pages if you wish, or you can add pages to the front matter, such as a list of your published books and/or "Praise for" pages with short review excerpts. I place this type of material before the title page as do traditional publishers.

TIP: Use section breaks between the elements of your front matter to maintain proper spacing. This also allows you to add page numbers when you come to the body of your story. If you want page numbers in the front matter, use Roman numerals.

Add alternating headers, placing your book title on the right-hand pages and your author name on the left.

Regarding font styles, the CreateSpace conversion

program doesn't recognize all fonts, so it's best to stick to standard ones unless you want to have problems.

I use Times New Roman 12 point for body text, varying sizes for chapter headings and in the front matter. Bold and italics are okay. Be careful to check your font for headers. Make sure you're consistent.

After you upload your formatted manuscript and it goes through the CreateSpace automated print check, view your book page by page using the Interior Reviewer.

If CreateSpace catches formatting errors, you will need to fix them and re-upload. This can be time-consuming, but it's worth the effort. In case you can't figure out the glitch, email or call CreateSpace Support. They are extremely helpful with any problems you might have, so you have a full support team working for you when you publish.

NOTE: Formatting your book for CreateSpace, as well as uploading it to CreateSpace, can all be outsourced on Fiverr. If you want the best-looking results, hire someone to do the formatting for you. Many providers can also include a Kindle version.

COVER:

Choose a finish for your book cover, either matte or glossy. This is up to your preference; either is fine.

Next, choose how to submit your book cover. There are three methods:

1. Build Your Cover Online with Cover Creator, a free CreateSpace tool to design your book covers.

2. Professional Cover Design, starting at $399. (Not recommended)

3. Upload a Print-Ready PDF Cover: CreateSpace provides detailed instructions for this method. If you did your own cover or outsourced it to Fiverr, this is the option you will use.

Using Cover Creator: Choose from several pages of pre-made CreateSpace cover designs (below on left) or design your own cover using a blank template (on right.)

First, design the front cover (can be done offline) making sure your image has a DPI of at least 300. Anything less than that will be rejected by the CreateSpace program.

After the front cover successfully loads, design the back cover. Include:

- a short, catchy blurb
- short review excerpts
- an author photo if you wish
- your publishing company name and URL

Look at the back of paperback books for ideas, and be careful to leave space for the barcode and trimming, as per CreateSpace instructions.

Lastly, set up the spine.

COMPLETE SETUP:

Review your project setup. If everything looks okay, submit your files for review. You can go back and make changes if you need to. When ready, submit for review.

REVIEW:

The CreateSpace automated review program makes sure your book is kosher for "manufacturing and cataloging." If it is, you will be asked if you want to order a proof copy for your final approval. You can buy the proof at your special publisher's cost.

IMPORTANT! I recommend ordering the proof so you can see what the final product will look like. No matter how much you edit and correct your digital book, you'd be surprised what kind of errors you'll find when you have the actual, physical book in hand. I cannot overemphasize this enough. You have to make absolutely sure that the book is good enough to show off to your friends and family. If there are formatting or editing errors in the book, it will reflect poorly on you, your publishing company and your reputation.

If you're okay with the book, you can have CreateSpace go ahead and publish it.

Do the following while waiting for the automated review to be completed (it may take several hours or longer).

DISTRIBUTION CHANNELS:

Choose distribution channels, including Expanded Distribution. Do NOT select Kindle. If you want to do a Kindle version, do so separately at http://kdp. amazon.com. Setting up a Kindle book is largely the same as a CreateSpace book.

DESCRIPTION:

Provide a description for your sales page. Assign a BISAC Category; add your author bio; set language, country of publication; choose search keywords; check for adult content if applicable and if you want large print.

PRICING:

Set a price for your book. This is what you will sell it for on Amazon. Use the built-in calculator to determine what the royalties will be. Keep in mind that distributors usually discount the book price, and Amazon will match the discounted price. If you set your price too low, you proceeds will suffer when the book is discounted. Of course, you don't want to price your book so high that it scares off readers. The $9.99 to $12.99 range is good enough for most applications.

Once you complete the entire process and approve the proof, CreateSpace will put it up on Amazon.

As soon as it is, you can send your prospects there to show them what you just accomplished. They can purchase a copy if they'd like. We're not trying to get rich off the book itself. We're using it to build credibility for your publishing company. By the way, when you send your prospects to Amazon, use your Amazon Associates link for yet another revenue stream.

When you notify your prospects that the book is ready on Amazon, congratulate them! Make it a big deal. Let them know that they can now show off their new book to their own clients. They and you should be proud of being on Amazon!

Need help with growing your offline marketing business?

Visit TrajectoryChange.com today!

CHAPTER 18: MONEY METHOD 2 – CUSTOM PRINTING

Other than the Wholesale Method, what are some other ways you can generate income?

Before we get to that, remember when I said not to fret if they don't place a wholesale order? Here's another way to entice them to make that wholesale order.

If they don't bite on the first offer, you can deploy Non-Buyer Email 1:

```
Hi {FIRST NAME},

Thanks again for contributing your
interview answers to "{BOOK TITLE}." As
our way of showing appreciation for your
time and contributions, we'd like to
extend a special offer to you.

For a very limited time, while we are
between projects, we have the ability to
print a special edition of "{BOOK TITLE}"
that would feature you on the front cover.
This special edition can include a full-
color picture of you or your company logo
```

on the front cover. The front cover of this special edition would also highlight the fact that the book includes a special interview with you and your company.

There are no set-up costs to have this special edition printed. The only thing we'd ask is that you purchase a minimum wholesale order of this special edition at the regular wholesale price of "{BOOK TITLE}." We will also sell this special edition on Amazon.com at no extra cost to you.

As you might imagine, handing one of your prospective customers a paperback book that features you on the cover of "{BOOK TITLE}" can be an incredibly powerful way of increasing your sales.

To have this special edition printed, please reply to this email.

Thanks,

{FIRST AND LAST NAME}

Associate Publisher

{YOUR DOMAIN NAME}

With this email, you're offering to publish a "Special Edition" of the book with their name and picture/logo on the front cover.

If they respond to the email and tell you that they want to move forward, you'll need to do 3 things:

1. Set up a separate wholesale order page, specifically for that client. This page will not have a book cover image because you still need to produce it.

2. Deploy Non-Buyer Email 2.

3. Change your book on CreateSpace to reflect the new front cover.

So first, set up the new wholesale order page. Again, this should be a standalone page, and it shouldn't be accessible to the general public. Only the client you sent it to should be able to access it. There's no need to password protect it, but make sure only that the client gets that URL.

When you're done setting up that page, deploy Non-Buyer Email 2:

```
Hi {FIRST NAME},

Great! We set up a special wholesale order
page for your special edition of "{BOOK
TITLE}."

You may place your order by logging into
the following wholesale order page for
```

your special edition:

{URL FOR SPECIAL EDITION ORDER PAGE}

Once you've placed your wholesale order for your special edition, please send me an email with a full-color picture that you'd like included on the front cover of the book. This full-color picture can be a picture of you, your company logo, or anything else that you think would be appropriate for the front cover of the book.

Thanks,

{FIRST AND LAST NAME}

Associate Publisher

{YOUR URL}

The thing about CreateSpace is that nothing is ever final. You can modify your book pretty much at will. So when you make this offer to customize a book for a client, it's pretty easy to do.

Now, remember when I said to include a graphic or picture on the front cover? This is where it pays off. You can just swap out that graphic with the client's picture/graphic. Make sure, however, that what they give you is high-resolution. Otherwise, it will look pixelated in the printed book version.

Then, below the original author name you put on the cover, you can put something like:

"Featuring {CLIENT NAME/COMPANY}"

Here's a tip: do not play the design game with the client. Just swap out your graphic for theirs. You don't want to get in a situation where the client is asking you to change fonts, colors, layout, etc.

You can also offer this custom version to clients who purchased the original version of the book. If you choose to offer this, however, do so after about a month or two after they placed their last order, so they don't feel cheated.

Need help with growing your offline marketing business?

Visit TrajectoryChange.com today!

CHAPTER 19: PREPARING FOR THE UPSELL

Whether or not your clients placed a wholesale order, now it's time to focus on generating more income, but doing so in service to them to benefit their business.

The first thing we need to do is to find out what they need. That will determine what direction we should go.

Remember that when you sent your questions out, you also sent at least three "unpublished questions." These were questions to survey your interviewees in order to see where they are in their business and what things they might need help with.

As you're getting answers back, pay special attention to the answers to the unpublished questions. If the interviewees filled it out correctly, they are telling you exactly what to sell to them. These are samples of some responses that I've gotten in my campaigns:

- "I am a [business type], not a marketer. I need help with marketing."

- "My biggest frustration is not getting enough clients. They don't know how to find me, and I don't know how to reach them."

- "I need SEO because no one can find my website."

- "I wish I could reach more people."

- "Sales! I hate selling! Isn't there a way to get more customers without having to sell??"

- "My business runs perfectly well. Nothing keeps me up at night."

You can see that they range from the very specific to the very broad. But you'll find some themes in the answers collectively that will give you a feel for what your market is asking for. For example, if they say that they need more customers, you can either sell them leads directly or you can offer some kind of lead generation service via SEO or social media.

This information is pure gold! The answers they give are the most valuable data you can get as a business owner. By truly understanding what they're asking for, you can tailor solutions to them that they already know they'll need.

This is why this system is different from any other "make money" courses out there. If you have been following everything correctly, you should have a small list of prospects with whom you've built some kind of rapport or relationship, you have proven your credibility and trustworthiness, and they have told you exactly what problems they need solved for their businesses.

With that information, you now should craft an offer to them that is based on whatever services you've decided to provide. This will require a little savvy and creativity on your part. In most cases, the prospects will not have told you something straightforward like "I need SEO." They will have said things like "I need more customers." It's up to you to read between the lines.

There are dozens of ways you can do this. It's only limited by your creativity in structuring an offer and service. In the upcoming chapters, we'll go over several Money Methods.

Whatever you decide, here's how to get them started.

Deploy Upsell Email 1:

```
Hello {NAME},

Thanks again for your participation with
{BOOK TITLE}! I am truly honored that you
decided to work with us, and many people
will find your contributions to be very
valuable for them.

I did find something interesting in the
interview you sent back. You mentioned
that you {INSERT ONE OF THEIR UNPUBLISHED
ANSWERS HERE. DO NOT COPY/PASTE, RE-WORD
```

IT SO THAT IT FLOWS WITH YOUR MESSAGE}.
You also mentioned that {INSERT ANOTHER
UNPUBLISHED ANSWER}.

{CALL TO ACTION}

Thanks,

{YOUR NAME}

The point of this message is not to sell them your services directly from the email. You want to continue the rapport you built with them, and you don't want to ruin that by acting like a rabid salesperson after you've been more docile with them during the project phase.

The Call to Action in this message is up to you. You can ask them to reply to you or call you. You can also send them directly to a sales letter, video, or webinar. I recommend a webinar.

Notice also that you are inserting their actual unpublished answers into the email. This way, the message is much more effective because it's what they said to you. You're not telling them what you think they should do, which is what traditional sales and marketing does. We're doing things differently, remember? It also means that each email you send is highly personalized and almost guaranteed attention from the prospect, which should result in higher conversions than your average marketing campaign.

When they do respond, the angle you're using is that your publishing company has special programs exclusively for authors and project contributors to help them with the problems they mentioned in their unpublished answers.

What is the potential of upselling? Let's say you're offering a $2,000/month social media management service. Let's also say you have 10 interviewees that you published. Those are 10 of the hottest leads you'll find. You should be able to contact all 10 and have a conversation with them. If half of them take you up on your offer, you have $10,000 per month's worth of social media management clients. Even if you only close one of them, that's a $2,000/month client. Remember, too, that you should not have stopped contacting prospects for other projects, so you should have an ongoing source of fresh leads to convert. If you convert one per week, that's $2,000 per week that you're bringing in.

You can upsell them regardless of whether they bought your wholesale offer.

Need help with growing your offline marketing business?

Visit TrajectoryChange.com today!

CHAPTER 20: MORE MONEY METHODS

In this chapter, we'll go over high-level overviews of more ways to generate income from your book clients. Each method is a comprehensive topic on its own, but I will point out the resources you'll need to make it happen. All you need to do is pick one that suits you. Of course, if you're resourceful and crafty enough, you can come up with your own methods to sell. After all, by now you've established an excellent rapport with your book clients, so it shouldn't be terribly difficult to upsell them.

MONEY METHOD 3 – DIGITAL MARKETING AGENCY

A Digital Marketing Agency (DMA) is your run-of-the-mill local business marketing consulting company. You provide online services such as SEO, social media, PPC management, etc. to offline businesses to help them market their online presence.

To start a DMA, I recommend signing up with a white label provider of marketing services. A white label service provider is a company that will perform marketing services for you under your company name. In other words, it's basically outsourcing the fulfillment of your marketing services to another company, but that company acts as though they are your employees. That way, they can do all the work, and even correspond with your client, as if they worked for your company. Your client never knows that you're outsourcing the work, or what company you used to fulfill the services.

For a traditional DMA, create an account with Endless Rise (www.endlessrise.com). This is a company that provides outsourced marketing services such as SEO, PPC management, reputation management, web design, and social media. You can pick and choose which ones you want to offer a client. They have several packages that have different levels of services and price points. Their pricing is " wholesale" pricing, which means you get to decide what you want to charge the client. The difference between what you charge and their wholesale cost is your profit. The best part is, you don't have to pay Endless Rise anything until you actually sign up a client, and the client pays you. It's exactly like wholesaling on CreateSpace.

For more about how their process works, sign up for a free account with them and check out their training webinars. One of the most valuable ones is how to build a multi-million dollar DMA within 5 years. The potential of this kind of business is huge.

Once you determine what kind of services you want to perform and what your clients are asking help with, and then you can approach them with your upsell offer.

MONEY METHOD 4 – CREATE ASSETS

This is a method that piggy-backs on the DMA concept. Instead of performing marketing services for the client's website or other digital assets, you can create your own assets and perform the marketing services on them.

Here's an example. Let's say your client wants to have YouTube videos done for higher Google rankings. Normally, you would create the videos and upload them to your client's YouTube channel or website, and then SEO them. What that will do is improve the rankings of your client's assets. Instead, you upload the videos to your own YouTube channel or website, with links or contact information to your client's business, and SEO that. The rankings improve for your own assets. Your client still gets the same exact benefits as if you had optimized their sites. However, since you own it, you can redeploy it for a new client should you ever part ways.

MONEY METHOD 5 – LEAD GENERATION

This method takes asset creation a step further. If your

clients say they need more customers, you can give them exactly that.

Create your own lead generation websites, videos, fan pages, etc. Generate traffic to those digital assets and capture leads. You can then sell these leads to your clients. You can also use paid methods such as PPC advertising to generate the leads at a certain price per lead. Then you sell the leads to the client at a higher price. The difference between the two is your profit.

There are several ways you can structure this type of program:

Flat Rate – client pays you a set amount each month. In turn, you send them whatever leads you generate, no matter how many. You can guarantee a minimum number of leads per month, and anything above the minimum is free for your client. For example, you can charge $2,000 per month for a minimum of 40 leads. If you send them 50 leads that month, they don't have to pay for the additional 10 leads.

Pay-Per-Lead – client pays you a certain dollar amount per lead you send them. For example, if you charge $30 per lead and you send the client 100 leads, they pay you $3,000 for that batch.

Hybrid – client pays you a "retainer fee" for your services. The client then pays you per lead you send. For example, you can charge the client a retainer of

$500 per month. Then, for every lead you generate, they pay you $40 each.

This type of monetization strategy is very involved. However, it can be extremely lucrative. It also shields you in case you lose a client because you can sell those leads to one of their competitors.

For more information on this method, please see http://www.totalmarketingstrategists.com/leadgen

MONEY METHOD 6 – AFFILIATE

If you really don't want to deal with your clients on an ongoing basis, then instead of upselling them to one of your services, you can refer them to another agency and get an affiliate commission or referral fee.

There are many established agencies that will do all of the work your clients need done. They will pay you for referring the client. The difference between this type of arrangement and a white label arrangement is that the agency will contact and close the client on your behalf. That's right, you don't need to actually get on the phone and sell your client anything because the agency will do it for you! With a white label arrangement, you still maintain the client relationship. With the affiliate arrangement, you're basically turning the keys over to the agency, and the client essentially becomes theirs, but they pay you for it.

If you need social media services for your client, you can contact John Hollings at Social Mojo (www.social-mojo.com). John will get on the phone for you to help close a customer, and he can accommodate a wide variety of situations.

Another great company that does a host of marketing services, including SEO, mobile, social media, guest blogging, reputation management and more is AudienceBloom (www.audiencebloom.com). Jayson DeMers owns the company and is a really sharp guy. You can also talk to him and his staff about this type of arrangement.

This is probably the easiest upsell method, but it will also make you the least amount of money.

MONEY METHOD 7 – HIGH-END COACHING

If you're really passionate about helping your clients succeed, and you have the goods to help them do it, then high-end coaching is perhaps the most lucrative of all options. You can structure a coaching program however you'd like and charge premium fees.

For example, you can offer a 1-on-1 coaching program for your clients to help them grow their business and charge anywhere from $1,000 to $5,000 per month or more.

You can offer a group coaching program where you can offer your clients group training or mentoring sessions. The advantage of this is you leverage your time and can "see" many clients at one time. For example, your group coaching program can teach clients how to publish their own books, delivered via weekly webinars or video training sessions. You can enroll 20 clients for a 6-week training program, and each client pays $3,000 each.

For more information about structuring a coaching program, please see http://www.trajectorychange.com

CHAPTER 21: CLOSING THE DEAL

No matter what money method you're going to use, you need to close the deal. I recommend actually talking with the prospect over the phone, or even in person. It's not 100% necessary – you can try to do everything over email, or even via webinar/video sales letter, but the phone will increase your chances of making money geometrically.

Now, I hear what you're saying. You hate selling. And frankly, so do I. I was in the subprime mortgage business for years. It was not fun. Here's the good news. Because you've built up some street cred with your prospect, your phone call should be fairly low key. Here's the better news. You're already armed with the unpublished answers to guide your conversation. With that information, there's a certain framework you can follow to help you close the deal.

So here's how it works. You call them up, and you talk about the book launch. You congratulate them, thank them, and tell them how fabulous it has been to work with them. Then you transition with, "I noticed in one of your answers from the interview that you said [INSERT UNPUBLISHED ANSWER HERE]. Tell me more about that."

They will start talking about whatever issue you brought up. The more they talk about it, the more they get invested in it. If they don't say much, you need to guide the conversation so that they open up more. Ask them why they said what they said. Ask them what the problem is doing to the business, his family, his free time, whatever. Then you move on to the next thing they said. Spend a few minutes really digging up the true feelings and frustrations behind their answers.

otice that they should be doing most of the talking. All you're doing is "interviewing" them. Be their Oprah. Be natural, conversational, curious, and interested. Ease them down the path they are trying to go. Then you transition the conversation by asking them where they would like to end up. How do they see their business a year from now? What's it going to take to get there? How would it change their life when they do get there?

The key is, you have to really establish that gap between their frustrations and their desired outcomes. Make them really feel that pain.

At the end of the conversation, you tell them that you understand their frustrations. Would they like help with that?

That's it. That's your close. No crazy salesman tricks. If all went well, they should be asking you what you have in mind. At this point, don't blow it by saying, "I do SEO. I do social media. I do PPC." They don't care, and it might make them defensive because they've probably tried it before and failed. Everything we're doing is outcome-based, not product-based. So when you get to the part where you're explaining how you can help them, tell them about the outcomes they can expect with you.

Outcomes that are benefits to their business, not features of what you do. Outcomes such as increasing their customer calls without any additional effort on their part. Outcomes such as saving money on their PPC campaigns without needing a Ph.D. from Google. Not outcomes such as getting them to #1 in the search engines or writing 3 social media posts per week.

Within this framework, you don't have to sell, and you should be able to close clients regularly.

Need help with growing your offline marketing business?

Visit TrajectoryChange.com today!

CHAPTER 22: KEEP IT MEDIUM

Hopefully, you're still contacting your prospects and closing deals. Hopefully, you're also continuing to prospect, sending interview questions, and compiling products. If you are, you should be pretty busy with a continuous cycle of prospects coming into your funnel.

After the first cycle of prospecting/interviews/product/upsell is complete, you should be feeling a huge surge of momentum and a sense of accomplishment. Don't lose this feeling. Carry this wave for as far as it will take you.

This is an important chapter because I've seen many people who have failed after achieving a significant milestone in their businesses. They stopped doing what brought them success (for example, continuing to prospect), or they took themselves in a completely different direction that wasn't able to sustain the business (for example, becoming too focused on service delivery and not enough on increasing sales). I want to make sure that doesn't happen to you.

You know all the clichés about staying the course and continuing the path. Former Washington Redskins

Head Coach Jim Zorn used to say "keep it medium." What he meant by this is that you don't want to get too high after a victory, and too low after a defeat (the latter being critical for both fans and players of the 'Skins). By doing so, you keep your focus on your ultimate goal, whatever that might be. That's not to say you don't celebrate victories (or closed deals). You absolutely should. You should feel proud of your accomplishments and realize that getting that victory was not easy. It took hard work, effort, sacrifice, and fortitude.

So celebrate, but don't decelerate (hey, I like that! I should trademark it!).

Keep your focus and continue to follow the process, as I instructed early on in this course. You see, every sales cycle is unique, every prospect is unique, and every situation is unique. No matter how well you did the first time around, you're sure to encounter something different the second time around. No matter how poorly you did the first time around, you're sure to encounter something different the second time around. And the third time. And the fourth time. No matter what those challenges are, stay focused on your process goals, and "keep it medium."

If you're persistent enough, you'll get the results you're looking for. So for today, no matter where you are in the process, and no matter what obstacles you have encountered, keep your forward momentum of action going strong.

CHAPTER 23: OUTSOURCING

I hope by now that you see the power of this strategy. Approaching business owners, experts, and professionals becomes much easier when you're trying to help them get their word out instead of trying to sell them something up front. Building rapport and establishing a relationship occurs organically, which is crucial to upselling them later. It's true what they say — people buy from people they like.

I strongly recommend that you continue with at least 3 or 4 cycles, from prospecting to closing. That way, you get very familiar with the entire process, see what works and what doesn't, get a few sales under your belt, and experience most of the most frequent challenges you'll face over the course of conducting this business.

After that, it's time to consider outsourcing and scaling.

You can outsource any or all of the parts of this strategy, making it completely hands off for you. However, I wouldn't just hand over the keys to a virtual assistant right away. You should still stay involved in some aspects of the business so you can systemize it.

The first thing you should outsource is the lead gathering. Getting leads for emailing will continuously fill your pipeline. This is the easiest process to outsource, and a good assistant can gather thousands of leads per week.

Then, you can consider outsourcing prospecting. Once you have a winning email campaign that boasts consistent response rates, you can have someone else email for you. This is the easiest task to outsource. You can set up an email account for them to use, or if you are using software such as ReachOut (www.reachout.io), you can give them an account to use. They can monitor your inbox for responses, and you should have a set of canned responses for the most frequently asked questions. If there is a situation that your assistant can't answer, they can forward it to you.

By outsourcing the prospecting, you can focus more of your energy on closing deals and increasing your income. Beware, however, that you should still monitor all correspondence. You don't want to be so hands-off that you bypass building rapport with the prospect. It will kill your chances of closing later.

Next, you can outsource the product creation process; that is, everything from curating the interview answers to creating the finished product. I would not recommend doing this until you have a steady flow of consistent closes. Outsourcing these types of tasks can take a bit of an investment, both in time training and in money spent. However, if you're busy closing deals, that should be your top priority. The more time you focus on revenue-generating activities, the more you should outsource repetitive and non-revenue generating tasks.

Lastly, you can outsource the closing process by hiring salespeople. This is not something you should undertake early on in your business's life. If you think you can shortcut the entire process by taking on a salesperson from the start, you'll find it exponentially more difficult than doing the sales yourself.

The process of locating, hiring, and training salespeople is a long and expensive proposition. Unless you have a lot of experience with hiring and managing a sales force, do not go this way until you are very profitable and have completely systemized your business. But when the time is right to take on a salesperson, that person should also handle the prospecting (but not the lead gathering or product creation). If you have any sales experience, you know that it's often wise to separate sales prospectors and closers. However, in this case, it's easier for them to be the same person so they can build that rapport from start to finish.

Where do you find outsourcers? One of my favorite sources is elance.com. I've found many quality providers there, and if you look hard enough, you can find a true gem that doesn't cost very much but provides outstanding work.

For example, I found one outsourcer from Bangladesh, who extracts names and emails from all types of different sites and directories, and he does it for $3/hr. He can compile thousands of leads per week, and he's extremely reliable.

However, my new "secret" source for finding assistants is on easyoutsource.com. This is a site that lists assistants from the Philippines in a variety of disciplines, from general assistants to programmers to telemarketers and everything in between. The workers on this site are the cheapest you will find anywhere, even less than odesk or elance. That's both good and bad, because you might have to go through a few people to find a good one, but when you do find one, you'll pay a fraction of what you would've paid on the mainstream outsource sites.

Another blessing/curse with easyoutsource is that they don't really have a platform. Sites like elance have a platform that houses all your correspondence and communication to within their site. They also facilitate the transaction, so payments are made within their platform. The good thing about the platform is that they have fail-safes such as escrow, so that if the work being done isn't satisfactory, you don't have to pay. This is something easyoutsource doesn't have. The drawback to the platform is that they don't release any of the VA contact information until you've officially posted a job. I like to interview and chat with outsourcers before posting a job to see what's out there.

By not being on a platform, you can have a lot more flexibility into how you pay your VA in terms of method, amount, duration, etc. More importantly, all of the contact information is readily available. You can contact them, interview them, and see what they can bring to your business without committing any resources.

I'm working with a quality assistant now from that site. He works for me full-time, even on Saturdays, and I pay him $150/month, which is a lot for where he lives. Browse around easyoutsource and check out what kind of people you can find to help your business. You are sure to find a quality resource to compile leads and do the emailing/prospecting for you, as well as product creation.

Once you have systemized your business from start to finish, and you have outsourcers who are able to run the show for you, you can then scale your business. By this point, you should be generating enough revenue to hire more outsourcers. Training them should be easy because your processes should be systemized and repeatable. Then you can start producing several books per week, selling several wholesale deals per day, and upselling clients regularly. That, my friend, is the blueprint to a 6- to 7-figure business.

CHAPTER 24: NO LEAD LEFT BEHIND

To recap, you have learned to (and hopefully implemented):

- Start a publishing company

- Compile leads and prospect

- Interview and engage your prospects

- Create and publish a book

- Sell book copies at wholesale

- Upsell your interviewees into paying clients

- Outsource the process and scale your business

This is the cycle from start to finish. You should not stop after one cycle, and you must continually do the entire cycle pretty much on a daily basis. By doing so, you keep your sales funnel full of prospects, you're disseminating valuable information into the world for the public to benefit from, you're building goodwill with your prospects by showing them that you're spreading their message at no charge to them, and you're bringing in income from any clients you've sold.

Let's take it just one step further. Until now, I've only

guided you on upselling the prospects who have submitted interview questions. Indeed, they are the "low-hanging fruit" because you've engaged them the most, and they've handed you their frustrations on a silver platter.

What about the rest of your prospects? There's no reason not to upsell them, either, particularly those whom you've sent interview questions to but never received back. You'll find that the majority of interview questions you send won't be answered. That's okay and to be expected. However, just because they don't return the questions doesn't necessarily mean they're not interested. They were interested enough to ask for them. In many cases, they see the interview, decide to do it later, and eventually they forget all about it. Some may have been intimidated by the questions and decided not to do it after all. Some may have lost interest altogether.

Regardless of why they haven't answered, the fact that they haven't responded gives you every right to contact them back. They expressed interest; you sent them what they asked for, and since you haven't heard back, you're following up.

There are a few different directions you can take with this. You can try to get them to answer the questions for a future edition of your publication. You can try to get a referral to the appropriate person who might want to answer the questions instead. Or, my preferred method is to take them a different direction completely.

Instead of continuing down the publication route, I will ask them to attend a webinar. You can also send them to a video, sales letter, blog, or whatever information you want them to see. On the webinar, I will give them some valuable content to help them in their business, and then I'll upsell them directly from the webinar. If it sounds like too much work, the effort is well worth it for the potential payoff. You can shortcut the work by doing an automated webinar, so you only need to present it once, and then use software like the forthcoming EverWebinar to automate it.

This tactic will give you at least one additional stream of revenue, which maximizes the mileage you get from your prospect list.

CHAPTER 25: CONCLUSION

I hope you learned something that will help your business and that you found value in the teaching and support.

The last lesson I have for you is to take massive, imperfect action. You don't have to get it perfect before you start; you just have to start. In Silicon Valley parlance, you start lean, and then you iterate based on the feedback you get. If you find that your prospects are wanting for you to take them in a different direction, then you "pivot" and provide them what they're looking for. Many great companies, and many companies of greatness started out this way and will continue to do so for eternity.

I thank you most sincerely for joining me in this program. It has been a pleasure to walk you through this process, and I look forward to hearing about your success.

Need help with growing your offline marketing business?

Visit TrajectoryChange.com today!

ACKNOWLEDGEMENTS

This book is the result of all of the marketing knowledge and experience I've accumulated over two decades. Every success I've had is because of the lessons I was taught in business, in my career, and in life. I am eternally grateful and truly honored to have been the recipient of the wisdom and guidance of so many.

First and most importantly, I want to thank my dad, Lamberto, who passed his entrepreneurial spirit and drive on to me. My dream was to work side by side with you in growing the family business. Unfortunately, geography makes it a dream unfulfilled, but I carry your spirit in every endeavor. I work hard every day to build a legacy that began with you. I owe everything to you. Without you, there is no business.

The start of all of my ventures really began with Ted Ciuba. As a young, fresh-faced college kid, you taught me finance, sales, and business strategies. Even though you were a very successful direct marketer, you answered my phone calls and took the time to answer a kid's questions. I wanted so badly to be one of your success stories, and while I wasn't able to accomplish that, I still have your lessons programmed in my subconscious to this day. Thank you.

I would like to thank those who believed in me in the Information Technology world, where my corporate career flourished. You took a chance on me when I was supremely underqualified for every job you offered: Stan Gelbaugh, the greatest quarterback in my book; Margaret Shanahan, Jorge Linares, Jenn Turcios, David Chandler, Todd Turner, Darren Richards, Emil Opare, Ben Gilbert, Glenn Goodwine, Lars, Lee, Laura, Hahndorf, Mehti, Jim, and all the good people from Seneca who taught me the ropes.

Mary McGovern, Karen Rarick, Jack Bamba, Steve Alexander, Ron Alexander, Karen Forng, Frank, Rick, Alison, Ron, Shirley, Stan, Kevin, Richard, Steve, Kurt, Dennis, Jules, Tom, Sami, Zach, and Clyde at the American Red Cross. Showtime!

At the United States Senate SAA, thank you, Tony Skarlatos, for the opportunity. Thanks Dana, Kenny, Goren, Lobo, Daskal, Sukie, Eric, Moon, Detlef, the Judiciary Committee, Senator Clinton and staff, Senator Bob Graham, Senator Hatch, Senator Akaka and staff, Senator Biden and staff, the late Senator Kennedy and staff, Senator Lieberman and staff, Senator Carper and staff, Capitol Police, and all the guys and gals from the Russell Senate Office Building dungeon. RIP Dennis Gregg and my trainmate, Dan McGrath. Miss you dearly, my friend.

For allowing me the opportunity to move to Atlanta and the American Cancer Society, thanks Laurie Durr, Alvin Milner, Darrell Shaw, Ray Allen, Ken Lu, Shane Hicks, Will Metz, James Easterling, Ron Jackson, Thorston Thorpe, Dwayne Ladson, and Gabe Lewis. Thanks also to Marece, Stan, Yolonda, Debra, Josh, Hemanth, Kew, Barbara, Chuck, Jill, Landon, and Merv Weis. Thanks to my softball team for allowing me to coach you and putting up with my crazy rules: Jessica Pedraza, Tam Huynh, and all my teammates.

At BCD Travel, thank you, Mike Corujo. You believed in me and showed me tough love, more than any other. Thanks Chuck Gillmore, Daryl Williams, Charles Hamilton, Chris Cillo, Yuri Levenfeld, Mike English, Sherod Plowden, Tom DiLeo, Tripp Garvin, Todd Arrington, Reggie, George, Rod, Norm, A.J., Andre, Mohsin, Tim, Dan, and Orlando. Thank you to EMC, who made me look more competent than I was, especially James, Scott, Jim, Dan, Kowall, and Kathy.

In my online consulting career, there are far too many hundreds to mention, but I must acknowledge Marty Gallagher, who helped start it all. I am grateful for you, and you changed my life for the better. Wayne Longmore, Ken Richards, The Honorable Winston Chung-Fah and his wife Barbara, who are the essence of the word "coach."

Thanks especially to the online and direct marketing

greats from whom I've learned. None of this would have been possible without you. The influences on my business are too numerous, but I want to acknowledge in particular, and in no particular order, Brian Anderson, Michael Cooch, Mike Koenigs, Ed Rush, Syd Michael, Mark Helton, Lee McIntyre, Russ Ruffino, Armand Morin, Jeff Walker, Ryan Levesque, Todd Brown, and Kevin Nations.

Thank you to my new friends, masterminds, and partners Tommie Powers, Ryan McKinney, Usman Ahmad, Damon Greene, Devon Brown, Saul Maraney, Reed Floren, Shane Farrell, Bryan Harkins, and Mark Tandan. We're going to crush it!

A very special thank you to my Coalition. I am humbled and honored to have met you. Your incredible marketing prowess is only surpassed by your gracious nature: Joe Lavery, Henry Gold, Gary McCormick, Matt Stefanik, John Cornetta, Andrew Liles, Temper Thompson, Brian Evans, John Adams, David Wright, Sam England, Milton Brown, and those I have yet to meet.

My deepest and sincerest gratitude to the coaches and mentors who personally took me by the hand and had a direct impact on my business. Adam Spiel and Tony Tiefenbach, your knowledge and experience are truly inspirational. Lee Murray, you challenged my thinking and showed me a side of myself that I didn't know existed. Mario Brown, you drove me and pushed me beyond my limits, helping me break through my self-imposed barriers along the way. You are an inspiring coach, and being under your tutelage is one of the best decisions I've ever made. And finally, Matt Bacak. I've looked up to you for almost a decade. Your brilliance never ceases to amaze me. Thanks to you, I have grown personally and professionally in ways that never would have materialized otherwise. I am incredibly grateful to have you as a friend, ally, and mentor, and I look forward to following in your footsteps. You rock!

To the hardworking staff of SociaVerse Publishing, who are the engine that moves us forward.

My eternal gratitude goes to Anne Conlan, the coach who launched my star and changed my trajectory. The Hodgson clan, especially Mary, Chris, Amelia and Joe. The Davises and Tulls, thank you for your support. RIP, Pop.

Thank you to my extended family, Tito Bobby, Kuya Ronald, Kuya Robert, Tita Beng, Rosabel, Ricco, Joanne, Jean, Dimple, Anna, Alvin, Tita Baby. Tito Danny, Tita Violy, Tita Ched, Tita Lydia, Tita Angie, Tita Imelda, and Tita Amy. I miss you all so much. Gone, never forgotten, always loved are Nanay, Tatay, Olay, Oloy, Tita Lita, Tito Bernie, and Tita Nardette.

To Uncle Larry, thank you for being there, for having my back, and supporting me at my lowest. I can never repay you for all the help you've given me.

To Rino, my brother and best friend growing up. Thank you for being my biggest athletic supporter (ha!), my partner in crime, and my comic relief.

To Mark, my baby brother. Thank you for geeking with me, for the advice you never thought I listened to, and for being there when I need you. You're still under contract.

To my mom, Milagros. Your name means "miracle," and it's miraculous that I was lucky enough to have been brought into this world by you. Words cannot even begin to express how much I love you and how truly fortunate I am to have been raised by you. I could not have chosen a better mother. I'm sorry to have been such a pain in the ass to make you quit your job, but honestly, you didn't really want to work there anymore, did you? You provided for me, you bailed me out of the trouble I made for myself, and you supported me unconditionally. The best version of me is you.

And to my beautiful wife Bernadette and children Nico, Julianna, and Samantha. This has always been, will always be, for you.

ABOUT THE AUTHOR

Online marketing expert Lee Nazal has generated millions of dollars in revenue for his consulting clients, including coaches, authors, attorneys, non-profits, restaurateurs, churches, sports clubs, and other businesses.

A former "paperboy," his journey began when he was unemployed with only a part-time newspaper delivery job to pay the bills. He stumbled upon a life coach who helped him refocus his talents. This encounter launched a successful career in Information Technology and marketing.

His success has enabled him to travel around the world, embarking on adventures such as skydiving in Fiji, snorkeling in the Great Barrier Reef, paragliding in Switzerland, breathing air in Beijing and eating haggis in Scotland.

Because of the guidance he received during a low point in his career and personal life, he has made it his mission to help other marketers become as successful as possible so that they, too, can launch the star of someone who struggled as he did.

For more information, please visit www.LeeNazal. com.